Animatronics: A Designer's Resource Guide

Rodney Heiligmann Ph.D.
Gene Poor Ph.D.

Layout by
Travis Gillum

Animatronics, A Designer's Resource Guide
Copyright © 2003 by Rodney Heiligmann & Gene Poor
All rights reserved.
Printed in the United States by Image Graphics, Inc.

Published in the United States by
Ian Hunter Publishers

Distributed by:
Jem Communications Inc.
1225B Central Street
Evanston, Illinois 60201
1.800.877.1406

1. Animatronics. 2. Animation. 3. Exhibit design. 4. Theme park design. 5. Museum figures.

Designed by Travis Gillum

ISBN 0-9747455-0-2

Other books by Gene Poor include: *The Illusion of Life; My Brains Are In My Back Pocket; It's Your Dream, I'm Just In It; Everything I Know About VCT - So Far (Fits in My Back Pocket)*

Foreword

Ever since we published the first book on animatronics, "The Illusion of Life - Lifelike Robotics," we have been encouraged to write other books on the subject. People wanted more depth on the technical side. Some wanted to know more about how to build animatronics on their own. Others were intrigued by the skills of the people behind the animatronics. Still others were interested in how to incorporate animatronics into projects they were designing and building. It was this last inquiry that motivated us to write this book - the integration of animatronics into various exhibits and attractions.

Animatronic manufacturers traditionally have waited for designers and planners to incorporate characters into their projects creatively. And they have done so for the last 20 years. Some successfully. Some not so successfully.

It is our belief that you cannot be creative with a technology with which you are not familiar. It seemed to us that we needed to document some of the more successful applications so that designers and planners could better understand what made animatronics work from both technical and creative standpoints.

We also want to share what we've learned about the industries where animatronics are typically utilized. We have included some rules, laws, observations, hunches, and a few off-the-wall ideas to whet the design appetite.

Acknowledgements

There are several people whose talent and passion have taught us a lot about the animatronic industry. We would be remiss if we didn't acknowledge their contributions.

Mike Blasko
Scott Campbell
Bob Erekson
Susanne Fruland
Tom Kuebler
Lara McGlaughlin
Doug Mollsen
Tom Suter

Table of Contents

Introduction...	7
Ten Laws of Animatronics...	8
Attraction Callers - House of Frankenstein.................................	12
Attraction Callers - Marvel Adventure City..................................	14
Casinos - MGM Grand Casino...	16
Children's Hospital - Johnson Hospital..	18
Coin Op Machines - The Brain Fortune Teller.............................	20
Dental Office - Grand Dental..	22
Greeters - Toledo Zoo..	24
Miniature Dioramas - King's City...	26
Multi-purpose Display - NWTF Statue...	28
Museum - The Chisholm Trail Museum......................................	30
Museum - Wonders of Wildlife..	32
Museum - Earlyworks...	33
Museum - Early Man Exhibit..	34
Restaurant - Jekyll and Hyde Venues..	36
Retail Display - American Girl...	40
Retail Display - Jungle Jim's International Market.....................	42
Science Centers - Taipei Astronomical Museum........................	44
Science Centers - Health Royale...	46
Trailer-based Traveling Exhibit - M3 Marketing.........................	50
Stage Show - The Big Yummy...	52
Research - Ken Feingold..	56
Tradeshow - Rubbermaid..	57
Tradeshow - GenFlex..	58
Tradeshow - Honeywell..	60
Tradeshow - Vacuflo of Ohio..	64
From Tradeshow to Showroom - Midmark.................................	68
Things to Consider..	70
Things to Consider - Sculpting a Likeness.................................	72
Things to Consider - The Continuum of Animatronic Moves...	76
Things to Consider - Choosing Moves..	78
Things to Consider - Maintenance..	80
Things to Consider - Definitions..	81
The Process - Designing and Building an Animatronic Character.......	83
The Process - Sculpting..	84
The Process - Molding and Casting...	85
The Process - Fabrication and Machining..................................	86
The Process - Scriptwriting and Audio.......................................	87
The Process - Figure Finishing and Costumes...........................	88
The Process - Control Systems...	90
The Process - Installation...	91
The Process - Supporting Media...	92
Credits..	94
The Authors...	95

Introduction

This book is about entertaining, selling, teaching, and persuading. It's about getting people's attention so you can communicate something to them. Capturing someone's attention is one of the most difficult things designers must do because human beings are so varied in what interests them.

Our preferred method of getting people's attention is through the use of animatronic characters and shows. Over the past 25 years we've had the great fortune to partner with some of the best designers in the exhibit and attraction industries. And we've had a chance to learn from each of them. The result has been a string of truly incredible animatronic figures that have helped to redefine how animatronic figures are used today.

We have three goals with this book... We want to highlight some exceptional projects on which we have worked, we want to share some of the lessons we have learned, and we want to acknowledge the people behind those projects. We hope you enjoy the ride.

The Ten Laws of Animatronics

We've been studying what works and what doesn't work in animatronics for over 25 years. What we have found is that the animatronic characters that perform successfully are almost always in alignment with some fundamental notions. After years of studying and analyzing applications and characteristics, we have assembled our findings into ten basic laws that govern animatronic success and failure in the entertainment and educational arenas.

1) The law of distance

The greater the distance between the audience and an animatronic character, the more you can get away with in terms of believability. Distance will determine everything from the quality of skin and hair, to how many character movements are necessary to make the character believable. In the early Disney animatronic years, Walt would never let audiences within 30-40 feet of a life-like human character. Consider the early Lincoln attractions. Abe was located high on a stage – far removed from direct audience contact. Disney knew that Lincoln's early animatronic movements were not technically sophisticated, and distance would help masquerade those limitations - thus increasing believability. More recently, the Madame Tussauds attraction in Las Vegas' Venetian Hotel has installed an Elvis animatronic utilizing the Law of Distance - hoping to increase the believability of that character.

2) The law of time

The shorter the time a character is viewed, the less sophisticated an animatronic needs to be. Consider a typical animatronic dark ride application. If the audience is traveling in a moving car at a fairly rapid rate of speed, eye blinks and eye turns would not be a character requirement. Those kinds of movements would not be seen, appreciated, nor add to the experience. On the other hand, the longer a character is seen by an audience, the more sophisticated it needs to be. If the audience is watching an historic figure tell a two-minute story, the audience is going to notice if the eyes do not blink or the arms never move.

3) The law of numbers

The more characters performing and/or the more movements each character has will increase the total audience "attention" holding time. A single character can only hold an audience for a short period of time unless it continues to reveal new movements throughout the show (surprises). However, multiple characters allow interaction, and the variety of personalities generally increases the effective performance time. With multiple characters interacting, it is easier to set up a good versus bad or right versus wrong relationship. That relationship generally helps with Law #7.

This three move turtle interacts with up to seven other limited animated characters to carry a several minute show at Great Bear Lodges.

4) The law of non-human
Non-human animatronic characters are not judged as critically as human life-like ones. No one really knows what a talking beverage bottle, animated garbage can, or singing chicken is supposed to look like. Hence their movements are not judged critically by your audience. You can get away with fewer movements and take some real risks with what they do and say!

Dr. Baktylife and his dog Tripod had everyone talking at IAAPA '99 when they sang and grooved to the hit "I'm too Sexy."

5) The law of surprises
Revealing surprises helps keep an audience's attention. Those surprises can be additional character moves, special effects, or just some unusual animatronic acts. Garner Holt Production's "Wendell the Unicycle Rider" is still causing audience members to debate how the trick was really done. Garner would share that Animatronic Law #1 helped keep his secret safe by flying Wendell high in the air on top of an advertising sign. Other notable examples of surprises are Lifeformations' clown with his pelvic thrust and Disney's Will Rogers character that performed a lasso trick.

6) The law of singing
Audiences are addicted to animatronic characters that sing. There is something mesmerizing about things that sing but are not human. We have witnessed this phenomenon consistently in various venues. For instance, Honeywell asked Lifeformations to design and build an animated hospital operating room for a medical administrators' trade show – a relatively conservative audience to say the least. The booth stopped visitors dead in their tracks, and the message was burned into their brains with music and singing. People were leaving the hall humming the songs while singing Honeywell's praises. A side note – Honeywell gathered over 100 qualified sales leads during that show, compared to five the previous year!

7) The law of personality
Scripting, voice talent, and personality are critical to character believability. All of these components go hand-in-hand to form a character's soul. We urge clients to think first in terms of a distinguishable personality when conceiving an animatronic character. If the personality is not a given inherent quality, we then urge them to think in terms of famous personalities to reference. We often ask, "if your character could be a film or television star, who would it be?" That identification generally helps set the character design process in motion and makes both the scripting and voice talent selection easier. Be sure to use a script writer who understands the animatronic medium and a voice talent that can bring life and personality to the narration.

Giant Nazdar ink bucket with a Jersey tough-guy personality utilized the laws of scale, personality, and non-human.

8) The law of brevity

Brevity in performances is your best friend – leave audiences wanting more. We encourage clients to limit any presentation to a minute or less per character. This law is simply the most difficult for clients to understand. They typically have an hour of content to share. We constantly remind clients that audiences do not remember much. The secret to being a bore is to tell everything. Note: The law of brevity may be broken by carefully and skillfully incorporating laws 4, 5, 6, and 7. Remember – if the audience stays around for an additional performance, you have just received the equivalent of an Academy Award for Animatronic Performances.

9) The law of scale

Changing the size and proportions of things helps create audience interest and grabs their attention. For instance, make things that are small, bigger. A gigantic animated squid was built for a Disney attraction in Tokyo. This character very well may be the largest animated character ever built. Conversely, make things that are big, smaller. Lifeformations designed and built an animatronic talking house for Honeywell's trade show booth that stole the homebuilder's show. The six-foot-long house came alive and talked about all of the places in a typical home that Honeywell products can be utilized.

The giant jumping beans in the Big Yummy Show at COSI Columbus bouncing and tooting to a tune about food, utilizing the laws of scale and edge.

10) The law of the edge

If it's appropriate and possible, go over the top with your character – push the edge. The beauty of animatronic characters is their ability to do things that other media cannot and repeat that ability over and over flawlessly. We encourage clients to push the limits. Show people something they've never seen. Be audacious! Have the spirit of P.T. Barnum! It's show business. Make it funny. Make it crazy. Get their attention! Deliver the message! Risk nothing - gain nothing! Joan Rivers once said "Most stars play it safe because they have too much to lose. Superstars are the ones who throw caution to the wind, improvise impulsively, go for the high note. Superstars give it everything they've got and hold back nothing at all. In a word, the difference is guts." Have guts – get edgy!

Hugh Mongous entertains tourists in the Wisconsin Dells. His scale (eight feet tall in a seated position) definitely attracts attention!

Combine laws for dynamite results!

Playing on the old freak show theme, LifeFormations combined the laws of edge, surprise, scale, personality, singing, and numbers to take the Best of Show Award at the '01 International Association of Amusement Parks and Attractions show. The big surprise came when the cigar-smoking clown thrust his pelvis to the beat of the rap song he was singing!

Attraction Callers
House of Frankenstein

It is a longtime tradition in some types of businesses to place a caller in front of their establishments to guide people through the front door. One can still find this technique being used around Parisian restaurants, along Bourbon Street in New Orleans, and outside the haunted houses and wax museums of Niagara Falls. It is in this last location that animatronics have really increased the impact of the caller.

Clifton Hill, on the Canadian side of Niagara Falls may be the most concentrated two blocks of attractions anywhere in North America, and likely the world. Each attraction must attract the attention of passersby who know that if they miss this attraction, there will be another one just a couple of steps away. Current techniques for attracting some of the millions of visitors through the front door include licensing popular icons such as Marvel's Comic Book Superheroes or the Scooby Doo characters, and opening popular franchises such as Planet Hollywood or Rainforest Café. Despite this trend of licensing popular culture icons, the basic challenge of communicating what is inside the front doors still remains.

House of Frankenstein
The House of Frankenstein is a traditional haunted house relying on suspense, surprise, and clever effects to entertain its audience as they walk through the attraction. As a traditional attraction competing against brand-new multi-million dollar installations, House of Frankenstein needs to immediately communicate that it has something to offer that is unique on the hill.

The Figures
Playing to the name of the attraction, owner Ian Paul wanted to recreate the story's scene where the mad scientist brings the creature to life. Ian also wanted to add humor to the suspense of the story to attract a broader crowd.

The scene was designed to be an amalgamation of different suspense and horror icons. The scene was created around the creature, which is strapped to the operating table. The scientist is a rotting zombie who stands at a control panel while applying various amounts of electricity to the creature. A human skull sits on a stack of shelves holding books, beakers and other mad scientist items enticing his master to apply more electricity to the creature's brain.

Short scripts and singing between the scientist, monster and an animated skull help draw the tourists inside.

The Objectives
The scene was essentially a caller for the attraction designed to meet two objectives:

1) Pull people into the attraction.
The scene had to stop people in front of the attraction. The script was written to move very quickly between lines suggesting suspense, classic horror, and a bit of humor within the time it took to walk past the window. A song was also included as a means of holding the audience long enough to get them emotionally invested in the attraction. The script passed quickly between characters, to keep the audience physically looking around the scene. The movement of the figures was programmed to highlight different moves with different lines to keep people interested longer – waiting to see something they had not seen earlier.

2) Establish expectations and good will.
The scene had to establish achievable audience expectations so word of mouth for the attraction would be positive. Everything about the style of the characters, set work, and script had to reflect the style of scenes one could find inside – which were basically the style of early horror films. The figures were created with muted browns, grays, and greens. The scene played like a movie trailer for an upcoming attraction. Everything looked to be coated in dust and decay and the props were sparse but purposeful.

Attraction Callers
Marvel Adventure City

The Canadian Niagara Group recently opened Marvel Super Heroes Adventure City. This is a multi-million dollar project featuring rides and games, along with a retail center selling Marvel merchandise. Given the current popularity being enjoyed by Marvel and its superheroes and villains, the fidelity and integrity of the figures had to meet extremely high standards.

The Figures
A scene was created for the front of the attraction that featured Ultimate Spider-Man hanging from the ceiling of the entryway, while the Green Goblin floats up and down on his glider blowing smoke everywhere. Every few minutes they engage in a battle for people on the street to witness. Lights flash, smoke billows, and insults fly. At the end of the exchange, they invite people inside where they will finish their altercation.

The Objectives
The Spider-Man and Green Goblin scene was designed to meet two objectives:

1) Draw people into the attraction.
The location of the figures was down at street level, as opposed to up on a stage. This allowed the audience to become actors in the storyline – caught in the crossfire of the battle between the two characters. The storyline was left open ended, with the Spider-Man and the Green Goblin agreeing to finish the battle inside the attraction. The visitors were of course invited in to witness the conclusion of the storyline.

2) Represent the popular Marvel characters.
Obviously the physical appearance of the figures – the sculpts and the costumes - had to match the established characters. More challenging, however, was to create believable movement for the figures. The budget didn't allow for animated figures with fully articulated armatures. Borrowing from the classic gun fighter scenes, the figures were positioned in their equivalent of a stand-off. The Green Goblin was positioned on his glider under an overhang. Spider-Man was positioned hanging down from the ceiling on a web, believing he had cornered the Green Goblin. For both figures, subtle movement while staring at each other during this confrontation were consistent with audience expectations of the movement that would occur during a stand-off.

Casinos
MGM Grand Casino

Casinos are among the most sensory-rich experiences in the entertainment business. They are a constant stream of sights and sounds, all designed to keep the patron in a constant state of excitement. One casino staple is the slot carousel – a row or circle of slot machines that are linked electronically together, typically playing for a common prize like a sports car or big money jackpot. Casinos continually try to outdo each other in the prizes they offer in these carousels.

It is known that an automobile placed in the center of slot carousels will generate more play per hour for those slots than slots simply lined up in a typical casino setting. Unusual treatment of graphics and machine design also affect game play. A few years ago, an experiment with several gnome characters was conducted at the Sands Casino to test the idea that animated figures would increase gambling. The characters did increase slot play by a third. As a result, several figures were created for the MGM Grand Casino slot carousels. More recent installations at other casinos have included a slot carousel with a Southwest theme including wolves that howl in celebration of a win, and a bovine themed *Moolah Mooing Cow* slot carousel.

The Figures
Gnomes
Seven gnomes were interspersed throughout an enchanted forest themed slot carousel. At the center of the carousel was a community prize – usually a car. The gnomes hid behind branches or next to waterfalls. Some held magic wands, while others had buckets of magic dust.

The Wolves
Three wolves appeared to be climbing around a rock mountain in the center of the slot carousel. When players won, the wolves howled to let everyone know.

Moolah Mooing Cow
Moolah celebrated each player's wins by mooing to the entire area.

The Objectives
1) Keep people interested in the slots.
Obviously the return on investment for these characters was their ability to keep people interested in the slots. To achieve this with the gnomes, three modes were created: 1) encouraging - they would pop up and offer words of encouragement or a helpful spell if someone had not won in a while;

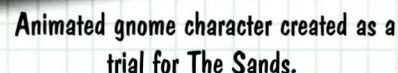
Animated gnome character created as a trial for The Sands.

2) celebration – they would pop up from their hiding places and celebrate when someone won; and 3) big celebration - they would all come up and sing if someone won the community prize.

2) Attract new players to the slot machines.
One of the few physical aspects of the gaming devices a casino can alter is the overall appearance. The more attractive or unique that a casino's slot machines appear, the greater the chance of attracting new players to the games. Casinos have designed their slot machines around a number of popular themes including Monopoly and Elvis. Some casinos have even based them on animals and have included animatronic wolves and cows that would celebrate a big win.

The Tin Man and Munchkins, created for the MGM Grand Casino experience

Children's Hospital
Johnson Hospital

If you were to create a short list of locations that could benefit from characters entertaining and interacting with people, certainly a children's hospital would make that list. And with the typical stereotypes of what a hospital is like on the inside, the potential to surprise people with really well designed characters was incredible.

Johnson Hospital in New Jersey needed to dress up one of the public areas of the hospital. The goal was to create several elements that patients and guests could enjoy, without interrupting the day-to-day operations of the hospital. Several animals in an African art style, both animated and static, were designed by COSI Studio. The animated figures tell jokes, short stories, and call out the time throughout the day. The static figures house interactive games.

Animated masks incorporate playful and inviting expressions and voices.

The Figures
The interactive figures
A turtle allows visitors to play tic tac toe on his belly through touch sensitive copper plates which activate fiber optics in the squares. A giraffe calls out guests' heights when they stand under her head. A snake uses lasers to allow guests to play his harp. A monkey makes different sounds when touching different fruits in his hat.

The masks
Elephant, rhinoceros, and hippopotamus masks hang on a wall where they entertain guests throughout the day.

The Objectives
1) The characters must not scare even the youngest of children.
With any show, the audience must be defined very early in the design process. In this case, the goal of the characters was to cheer up patients and visitors in the children's hospital. The finished product was intended to make the visitors' stay as enjoyable as possible. The storybook and arts and crafts style of the characters made them attractive to the younger crowd without threatening or scaring them.

2) The characters can be touched, but cannot hurt anyone.
Given the location, there was not room to create display work that could keep people from touching the characters. The overall textures and color patterns assured that any nicks or scratches could be touched up relatively easily and without calling attention to themselves.

Where there were moving parts, two techniques were used to greatly reduce the risk of pinched fingers: 1) the air pressure used to actuate the potential pinch moves was set very low; and 2) at the locations where a pinch was possible (e.g., corners of the mouth), foam and cloth were used and painted to match harder, more durable shells covering the rest of the figures.

The near-life-size African art themed giraffe reports the heights of visitors as they stand under her nose.

Coin Operated Machines
"The Brain" Fortune Teller

The Brain - ready to offer his infinite wisdom – that is if he can get his contraption to work right!

Return on investment is something that most companies and institutions consider with just about everything they buy. Sometimes that return on investment is simply educating or informing an audience. Sometimes it is selling general admission tickets. Other times, it is a much more direct cause-and-effect relationship, as with a coin operated machine. And the expectations can be pretty high. Some food/arcade venues expect their coin op machines to pay back their investment directly within 15 weeks. Some put the machine within a broader context, counting increased audience traffic and food sales in their return on investment. Fortune telling coin-ops are typically judged by the latter criteria because they are able to offer entertainment for more people than just the person putting the money in the machine. They can contribute to the overall atmosphere and identity of the location.

Machines that feature animated figures have been around for centuries. Originally featuring automatons, these machines had small figures of humans and animals performing some very difficult feat. In the late 1800s, fortune machines became very popular because they gave the audience something that cost very little, but was valued comparatively high: a fortune. Fortune telling machines in the later part of the 1900s introduced animated characters with synchronized mouth movement, allowing the machines to deliver a fortune without requiring a card to be dispensed. The arcade business is still seeking the next evolution of this machine, and at least one recent model has certainly deviated from the standard look of a typical fortune-telling machine.

The Figure
The Brain is the all-knowing, all seeing fortune teller whose scientific machine helps him perceive the future. Locked in his cabinet, he turns dials that cause sound effects to play, lights to flash, smoke to billow, and gauges to jump. The problem is, he is not that good. In fact, he would rather insult his patrons than tell them their future. In the end, his machine invariably breaks down and he is left to offer some feeble bit of advice, if that.

The Objectives
1) Create a new look for the fortune telling machine.
Traditional animated fortune tellers have looked like either old witches or old warlocks. If a new fortune telling machine were going to be successful, it had to look and sound different. The animated figure took the form of a mad scientist with an oversized cranium. The machine itself looked like an industrial conglomeration of spare parts, broken circuits, and surplus light bulbs. And the voice was a very obnoxious, gritty voice that barked at the patron. The ability of this figure to tell fortunes was very questionable.

2) Create a machine that attracted people to it.
While traditional fortune telling machines had signs and the occasional light on top of the cabinet, The Brain included several dynamic effects that would catch a potential patron's eyes. The neon flashed on and off as the machine sounded like its electrical circuits were going to overload; smoke billowed out of the top at the end of each 45-second show, and strobe lights fired within the cabinet as the sounds of a meltdown were played.

3) Create a machine that encouraged replays.
One of the problems with fortune telling machines that actually give a fortune is that people tend to think they should have only one fortune at a time. One play is all they will do. But, if the fortune telling machine does not actually give a fortune, if it insults the patron or tells them what their favorite vegetable is instead, then they will have a reason to play it again. The fact that the machine does things other than provide a fortune causes patrons to encourage their friends to play because it is so different from what people expect. They want to share the emotion of shock and surprise…two common entertainment emotions.

One of our favorite coin op venues
Every inch of Marvin's Marvelous Mechanical Museum's 5,500 square feet of floor space contains an array of buzzing and clattering vintage coin-operated devices; overhead dangle signs, animatronic dummies, over 40 airplane models gliding along a steel rail, vintage fans of all types, and classic sideshow posters. Located in Farmington Hills, Michigan, Marvin's is listed in the World Almanac's 100 most unusual museums in the U.S.

Traditional fortune teller with ultra-realism.

Dental Office
Grand Dental

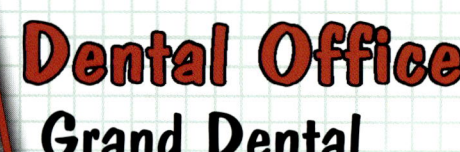
Gumper shows off his pearly whites.

Nobody likes to go to the dentist, least of all children. Major reasons for this include being afraid of the processes and not understanding the need for regular care. Overcoming these reasons is a constant challenge for dentists around the world. Many of their efforts have been limited to materials trying to explain the importance of taking care of one's teeth. While these may be factually accurate, they do little to entice people to read them, or overcome the fears people have.

Two Chicago dentists wanted to create a dental practice that not only decreased anxiety about visiting the dentist, but actively promoted the benefits of taking care of your teeth. When they remodeled their main office several years ago, they wanted to create a lobby that put their patients at ease about their visit. And if they did it right, the lobby could even make patients look forward to their next visit.

The Figures
Gumper
An imaginary figure that lives in a plant-covered hill created in the middle of the lobby. Thumper is about 15 inches tall, covered in fur, and has a soft squeaky voice.

Brush
Sidekick to Gumper. He has fiber optics in his teeth to show how brushing can make teeth sparkle.

The Objectives
1) Put the patients at ease.
The characters needed to be non-threatening, so it would not have worked to have a hero and villain. Instead, the stories centered around Gumper and Brush practicing good dental hygiene. The topics focused on the benefits of good dental hygiene, rather than focusing on the consequences of bad dental hygiene.

2) Introduce topics to be reinforced later.
As these characters were placed in the lobby, they were part of a controlled sequence of events…wait for the dentist, then talk to the dentist. The characters capitalized on this by introducing general topics about dental care with just a few details. Once with the dentist, the dentist then brought up those topics, filled in some more details, and quizzed the

patients on what they had heard. This reinforced the message in the patient's mind. And in some cases, the patient went back out to the lobby to wait for someone they had come with, giving them one last session with the material.

Gumper relieves tension in the dental waiting room for both young and old.

Greeters
Toledo Zoo

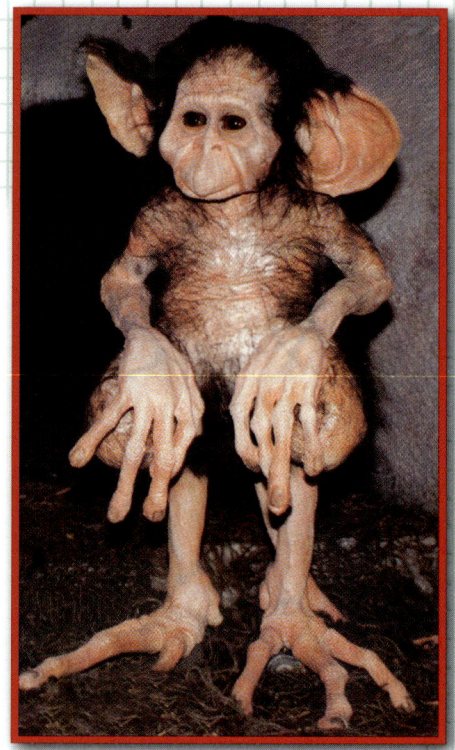

The Leapiguar

As discussed elsewhere in this book, one of the key advantages of animatronics as a communication medium is the ability to create them in any form. While this feature is often put to good use in theme parks, it is underused in more traditional settings such as museums and zoos. These types of settings, however, are perfect for animatronics to become teachers of important content.

The Toledo Zoo wanted to communicate how animals adapt to their environments and why they have the characteristics they have. The ultimate solution was to create a fictitious character with very exaggerated features. The Leapiguar was born. He welcomed people to the adaptation exhibit and explained what adaptation was, based on his own features.

A few years later, the Toledo Zoo wanted a new animatronic greeter for one of its exhibits. This time, the goal was to make children feel connected to the animals in some way, as though they could be friends. A boy figure was created that had an owl on his shoulder and a frog in his pocket. They welcomed people into the exhibit, showing that people and animals interact well together.

With the success of the exhibit greeter, the Zoo decided to create a greeter for its new gift shop. A baby polar bear figure was created and placed atop an iceberg kiosk directly in front of the store. The sound was piped out to the sidewalk so that people would turn and see the bear.

The Figures
Leapiguar
With most of his features exaggerated, he explains how his environment caused him to look the way he does. From his huge ears to his long fingers, his body parts encourage visitors to guess what advantages each of his features has.

The boy
He stood on a box to raise his height to be more crowd friendly and hide the control system. His bird has just enough movement to appear alive, and the frog has just one leg sticking out of the pocket with a single move that makes it look as though he is hopping around in the pocket when he talks. The dog speaks and moves his head in several directions to address the crowd.

The polar bear
Mounted above a display to greet visitors as they entered the gift shop. The merchandise kiosk below him held featured items.

The Objectives
1) Leapiguar had to be scientifically possible.
Because the Leapiguar was to be used in a zoo exhibit discussing adaptation, it had to be scientifically possible for his features to exist. While his existence was justified as being a visitor from far away, each of his features existed on common animals. Supporting exhibit material highlighted other animals that had similar adaptations.

2) All figures had to be adaptable for other exhibits.
The zoo's investment in the figures was made with the understanding that the figures could adapt to work with other exhibits. For several years, the figures have been reprogrammed to host holiday parties, meet VIPs, and serve as greeters to various new exhibits.

Little boy Max with his friends the owl, dog and even a wiggling frog in his pocket.

Miniature Dioramas
Kings City

Created properly, miniature dioramas can portray an event or scene in such a way that it has the same impact a full size scene would have on a viewer. The advantage of a miniature scene is that it can usually be created for a lower price and require less floor space to exhibit. The drawback, of course, is that miniature scenes allow fewer people to view them at a single time.

Miniature scenes/dioramas typically involve closely layered planes of figures and scenery, each in a different scale. The closest layer has the largest scale, and the layer furthest away has the smallest scale. The result allows an 8 foot deep diorama to appear to cover hundreds of feet of scenery. A mural along the back wall can help complete the illusion.

King City was looking for a way to show visitors several scenes from the Old Testament. The ultimate design took visitors on a walking tour through a maze of caves, with several dioramas tucked into the walls of the caves. A push button allowed visitors to select the appropriate language for the narration.

Forced perspective, as shown here in the arc scene, helped to increase realism in a confined space.

The Figures
The figures portrayed scenes such as the Garden of Eden, the Pharoah's Dream, and Moses with the Ten Commandments. To help create the illusion of depth, the height of the figures ranged from 1 to 24 inches tall.

The Objectives
1) Maximum movement in minimum space.
To create the illusion of a living scene, most of the characters were animated. For the 24 inch figures, this was accomplished with the same processes used to create the figures that are traditionally used for larger scenes. For the smaller figures, however, many of the moves were driven with levers and cables connected to cylinders hidden below ground level.

2) Timing the visitors.
Given the relatively small audience that can view the scenes at one time, it was necessary to motivate the audience to move onto the next scene in a timely manner.

The shows within each of the scenes along the path were timed to match each other. Show lighting dimmed at the end of the script to essentially make the scene hidden between shows, further indicating to the audience that they should move to the next scene.

Limited space in the smaller characters forced some movements to be driven externally, as with this scene where the pry bar is actually moving and the characters are just riding along.

Multi-purpose Display
National Wild Turkey Federation - Bronze Statue

One of the great aspects of animatronic figures is their ability to look like an inanimate object, and then shock the audience when they come to life. This shock forces people to stop, stare at the figures for a while, and then reconcile in their mind what their eyes are seeing. And while they are staring at the figures, they are listening to the message being delivered. The emotional response of shock or surprise helps define the moment in their minds, making that moment and that message more memorable.

Bronze and stone sculptures are particularly effective for this technique, because everyone is used to seeing these types of sculptures. They are not, however, used to seeing them come to life and move around.

NWTF Legacy Statue model with final life-size animated version.

The National Wild Turkey Federation needed an exhibit piece that could communicate the tradition of their organization. It needed to attract an audience while reflecting the culture of the organization. This piece also had to be portable so it could travel to trade shows and special events, but it also had to look proper sitting in a museum surrounded by high quality cabinetry and media exhibits.

The Figures
It was decided that the piece should be a life-size version of a 12-inch bronze statue the NWTF had previously commissioned. The statue showed a father, son and daughter walking through a field after a turkey hunt. The life-size version of the statue had animated heads and arms. These flexible heads and arms attached seamlessly to the more structural shells of the body and legs. The entire piece was painted to look like a bronze statue. Every 5 minutes or so, the statue would come to life.

The Objectives

1) Communicate the values of the NWTF in a non-lecture style.
The NWTF did not want people experiencing the exhibit feeling as though they were attending a lecture. They wanted the feeling to be casual and dignified. The three figures bantered back and forth with the father explaining some of the values championed by the NWTF. The movement of the figures was enough to keep the audience's attention for about 1 minute, so several 1-minute scripts were created, each one highlighting a specific part of the NWTF message.

2) The characters had to fit through a standard double doorway.
While the NWTF does attend large trade shows, they also have many events in smaller banquet hall facilities. To capitalize on their investment in the characters, they wanted to be able to take the figures into these types of settings. The entire piece was created on a single base with casters so it could be easily rolled down hallways. The overall size of the piece was just small enough to fit through a double door.

3) Hide joints between materials.
The surfaces of the statues were made with two materials. Wherever the figures had to move, such as their head and hands, silicone rubber was used. Wherever the figures did not move, fiberglass was used. While the artists were able to match the look of the two materials, the seam between the two was evident. To overcome this, the clothing was sculpted to create wrinkles with a blind side to them. Around the neck, for example, the shirt collars were made thicker, and pulled slightly away from the body to allow the silicone rubber to dive behind it on the blind side.

Other "precious" metals and stones...

The materials used to make animatronic figures can be made to look like just about any material that would be used for a statue or carving. Granite and marble busts are often brought to life. Sandstone and granite treatments are used for other sculpts such as ancient temple gods. Carved wood treatments have been used to bring several objects to life, including a 3 story tall toy horse.

The Chisholm Trail Museum

Storytelling has long been a method of passing information from one generation to the next. Animatronic figures are able to combine great stories with a passionate storytelling voice, and consistently deliver it to audiences day in and day out for many years. This technique has been particularly effective in history museums that want to put their artifacts into context for their visitors.

The Chisholm Trail Museum tells the story of how Jesse Chisholm began regularly using a route between grazing fields out west. Ultimately, others began using it until it became the preferred passage through Oklahoma. The museum wanted to tell this story from Mr. Chisholm's perspective. An animatronic figure was created so visitors could sit and listen to the story of how Mr. Chisholm established the trail.

Several years later, the museum was refurbishing several of its displays as part of an expansion effort, and decided to expand the animatronic exhibit. An animatronic partner was created for Jesse Chisholm, and the two figures were placed in a new themed environment.

The Figures
Jesse Chisholm
A seated character with moderate movement throughout the head and arms. He was seated to reduce the need for body leaning movement.

Tex
A younger looking character, his movement was limited to head moves and a couple of arm moves.

The Objectives
1) Create a natural storytelling situation.
One of the goals of the refurbished exhibit was to create a presentation that sounded like storytelling rather than lecturing. To achieve this, a second character was added that asked questions and spoke for the audience. This created a much more humble presentation of the story, in which Jesse is simply answering the questions of a young partner rather than boasting about his adventures.

2) Maximize the realism within the given budget.
One of the obvious goals of designers is to figure out how to maximize the effect of any exhibit component. When dealing with animatronic human figures, the designer must always be conscious of the fact that audiences are going to judge their performance against that of real humans. To help the animatronic figures withstand this comparison, designers will first figure out how much movement the budget can accomodate, and then try to put the figures in a gesture in which it will appear that they may only need a certain number of moves to look natural. In this scene, the Jesse figure is sitting in such a way that he would not make extravagant movements with his arms and body. Likewise, the casual slouch of Tex, with his arm resting on the saddle, looks very natural with a few head moves and only a couple of arm moves.

Designed for a camp fire scene, Tex is comfortably leaning on his saddle.

Storytellers...

"A picture is maybe worth a thousand words, but a good story is worth ten thousand pictures." Jim Lukasznewski

Stories are a powerful way of connecting with audiences. Stories are how we learn best. Stories are how we communicate best. Stories stir memories. Stories make us aware of shared experiences.

Good storytellers are irresistible. They can get attention any time and any place. Animatronics simply make great storytellers.

Museum
Wonders of Wildlife

Animatronic figures are often used in combination with other media, such as video. Sometimes this involves simply showing scenes or artifacts on a video screen that support what the animatronic is saying. Other times, however, the video becomes part of the scene. This allows the designers to dynamically change the scene or actors in the scene in a way not possible with themed sets or animatronic figures alone.

The Wonders of Wildlife Museum has exhibits relating to many types of wildlife and ecosystems around the world. In one of their exhibits, they wanted to highlight the social aspects of enjoying nature. A fishing scene was created, in which two friends are camping beside the river. One friend, the animatronic figure, is sitting by a campfire telling stories. The other friend, a video projection, is sleeping in the tent. The tent's front flaps are drawn back, revealing a rear projection screen on which the inside of the tent is projected. The video friend is sleeping on his cot. While the animatronic friend tells stories, the video friend jumps in to correct him, occasionally getting upset. Because he is a video projection of a real human, he is able to thrash around naturally in his cot when he gets upset. This balance between three-dimensional animatronic and two-dimensional video projection plays to both media strengths, and creates a very successful scene.

The Figures
Campfire friend
Sitting on a log, his position is very relaxed. One arm is resting on his leg, the other is poking the fire with a stick. The leg on which the one arm rests moves back and forth when the figure leans side to side.

The Objective
1) The scene should not appear to have "stopped."
This scene was located along a major walkway in the museum. As such, the museum designers wanted to make sure the scene never looked like it was turned off, or between shows. A standby program was created in which the figures had subtle movements, as if stoking the fire or glancing over at a noise in the nearby trees. When it was time for the show to start, the animatronic figure looked up as if he just noticed that someone was watching him. He then invited them to sit down and hear about his day.

In the campfire scene, a video projection of a person in the tent provided a more cost effective and dynamic alternative to a second animatronic figure.

Museum
EarlyWorks Museum Complex

While animatronic human characters are often used as storytellers in museums, there are many other types of storytelling animatronic figures that have been very effective. Large animated books, clocks, and dragons are just a few of the figures that have captured the attention of museum visitors with their stories.

A large turn-of-the-century city street was created at the EarlyWorks Museum Complex. It needed a couple of storytellers to explain what life was like back then, and relate it to today. Rather than create two human figures, it was decided to create a couple of figures that were a bit more unusual, but still appropriate for the setting.

The Figures
The tree
A very large oak tree with a face in the trunk. It is located in the middle of a town square, and invites people to gather around to hear stories of the town history. He has mouth and eye movements, and when he gets caught up in the story, he shakes his branches.

With its realistic bark and leaves, the inviting tree tells childrens stories throughout the day.

The clock
Standing high above the town crossroads, the clock face is proud to give direction to people. He has mouth and eye movements.

The Objective
1) Hold people's attention.
In this case, simply bringing everyday items to life interests people enough to stop and listen. These figures were created to have a storybook appearance to make it seem natural for them to be part of a story as well as inviting for children.

The animated clock face was seamlessly incorporated into a turn-of-the century style clock frame.

Museum
Early Man Exhibit

Most museums maintain an area within their facility to hold traveling exhibits. Hosting these exhibits allows a museum to offer its local audience fresh material on a regular basis. Over the past decade or so there have been several exhibits featuring animatronic figures, including dinosaurs, giant insects and even leaky body parts.

One animatronic-based traveling exhibit, designed by Danish company United Exhibits, featured the evolution of man over several thousand years. The centerpiece of the exhibit is a series of four dioramas depicting four different eras of evolution. Each diorama is hosted by a prominent scientist through a video presentation that is synchronized with the scene. As the animatronic figures depict their behaviors, the scientists interpreted what the behaviors meant.

Australopithecus figure using simple tools for gathering food.

The Figures
Australopithecus, Homo Erectus, Neanderthal, and Homo Sapiens were all created with limited to moderate body movement.

The Objectives
1) Scientifically accurate figures.
The purpose of this exhibit was to illustrate current theories of human evolution, the features of the figures from each era had to be very accurately created so that the audience could recognize and understand the evolutionary arguments being made by the scientists. Each figure was sculpted based on reference material approved by leading scientists, with the final sculpts also being approved by the scientific team. Skin colors and hair patterns were all based on current theories of how the early men and women looked.

2) No seams showing.
Two of the four dioramas featured cultures that had not yet discovered clothing. These figures, therefore, had all of their skin exposed. As to not detract from the audience experience, it was determined that seams could not be visible. This presented a challenge because the positions of the figures required the arms and sometimes legs to be created separately from the body. Additionally, the skins all had to be split to allow the animatronics to be put inside. The solution was to create very flexible strips of skin material that were applied over the seams after the animatronic components were installed and the figures assembled. The figure finishing process blended these strips with the existing body skin.

Like this Homo Erectus, most of the figures are full skin, which poses some movement challenges.

Restaurant
Jekyll and Hyde Venues

Restaurants have always had a tendency to theme their interior to enhance the experience of their patrons. A restaurant serving Italian food naturally incorporates some Italian architecture, photographs of Italy, and employee clothing reminiscent of Italian style. Historic or nostalgic restaurants have often tried to enhance their facility by including furniture and costumes that make patrons feel as though they have stepped back in time to the desired period. Recent decades have seen an explosion of such restaurants with themes ranging from rainforests to Hollywood movies. One of the most successful themed restaurant ideas has been New York's *Jekyll and Hyde Club* located in Mid-Town and *Jekyll and Hyde Pub* located in the Village.

The creator of the New York *Jekyll and Hyde* venues, D.R. Finley, developed an elaborate legend in which these establishments were founded by Dr. Henry Jekyll after fleeing London in 1931 to continue his search for a way to rid himself of his malignant alter ego – Mr. Hyde. Jekyll formed the club as a place to meet and house his artifacts while conducting research and experiments.

This legend serves as the guidelines and inspiration for pieces of themeing that are placed in the locations. Animatronics provide patrons with both a memorable experience and a reason to tell their friends about the establishments.

The Figures
Skeletons
Of course! These are the results of many years of experiments.

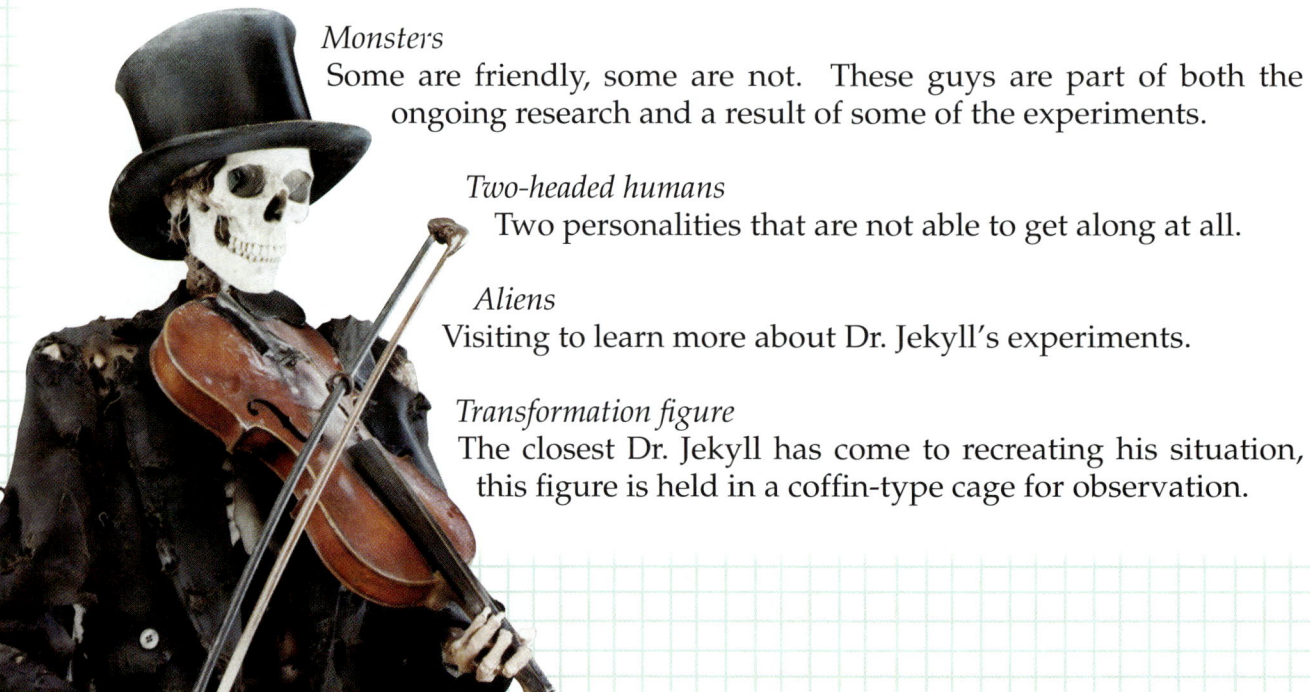

Monsters
Some are friendly, some are not. These guys are part of both the ongoing research and a result of some of the experiments.

Two-headed humans
Two personalities that are not able to get along at all.

Aliens
Visiting to learn more about Dr. Jekyll's experiments.

Transformation figure
The closest Dr. Jekyll has come to recreating his situation, this figure is held in a coffin-type cage for observation.

Skeleton musicians entertain the guests.

The Objectives
1) The animatronics had to appeal to adults.
While some restaurants target kids with their animatronics and hope their parents will follow, D.R. wanted to target adults. Restaurants prefer adult patrons because they eat more expensive meals and often order a drink from the bar (high profit). D.R. also knew that if he could appeal to adults, it would be successful with the kids as well. The animatronics are scary, slightly demented, and have supporting stories behind them. Their level of detail is much higher than most restaurant animatronics, encouraging people to explore their appearance to better understand their story.

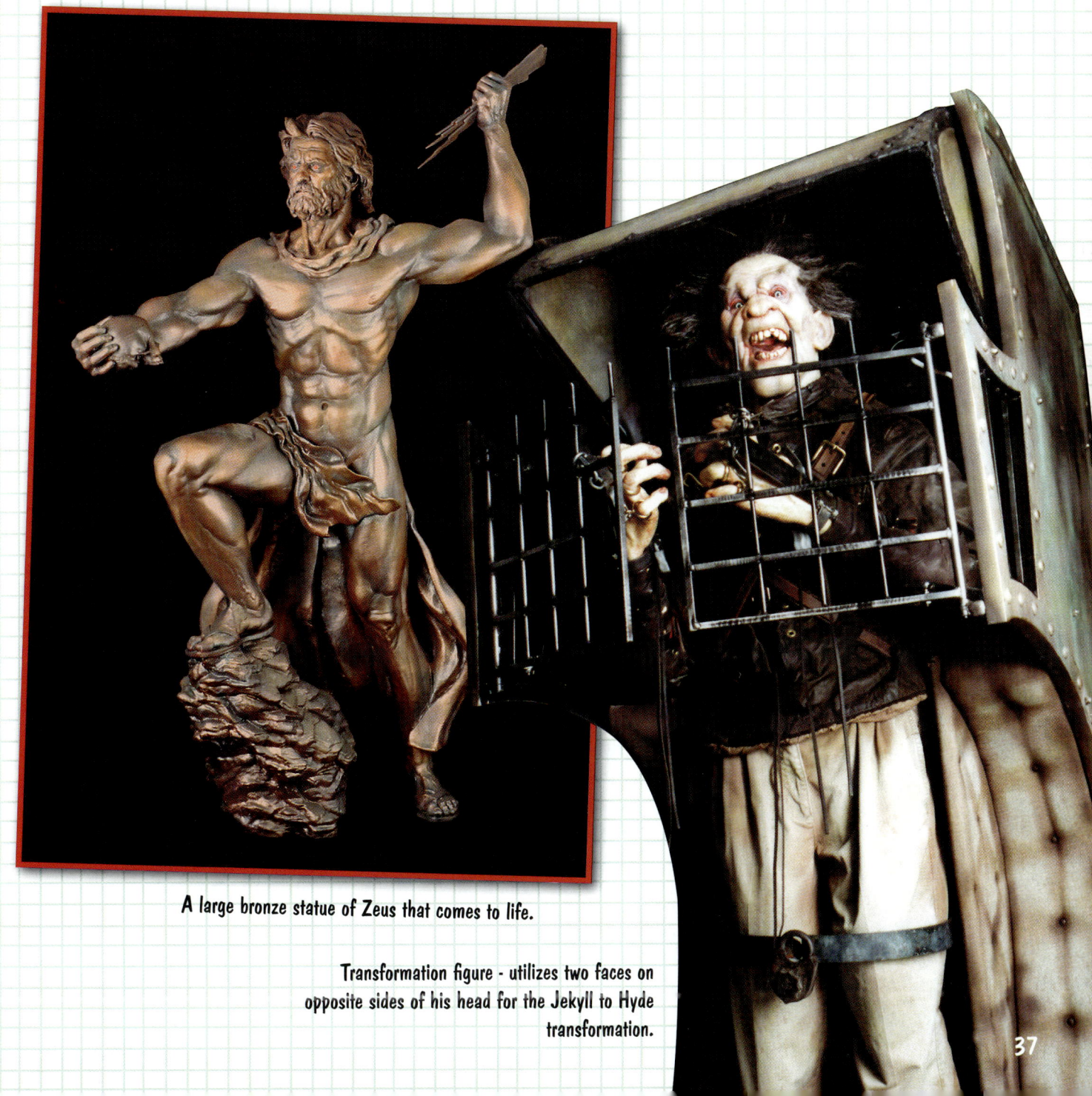

A large bronze statue of Zeus that comes to life.

Transformation figure - utilizes two faces on opposite sides of his head for the Jekyll to Hyde transformation.

2) The animatronics could not be predictable.
One of the unique aspects of the control system for these animatronic figures is that it allows them to be instantly switched from a pre-programmed show to a live operated show. This allows the personalization and spontaneity of a live performance to entertain patrons, and assures that each visit is somewhat unique to previous visits. Actors control the figures from behind the scenes, watching and listening through cameras and microphones placed at the figures.

3) The animatronics had to be part of the décor.
While many themed restaurants seem to buy a character out of a catalog and use it as a space filler, D.R. wanted the animatronics to appear completely natural within the layers of artifacts that cover the walls. Each one was custom designed to tell a specific story. Some were parts of experiments gone awry. Others are fellow scientists. And others are just visitors passing through. The set work surrounding the animatronics fills in the back story. The result is a décor that truly looks as though someone had been researching ancient artifacts or conducting experiments for the past 70 years.

Spaz the Gremlin and Slim Slaughter peddle their goods in the gift shop with Slim offering his shrunken heads at a "reduced" price.

Gunther Meaney - another figure which could be run live to keep the experience unique and fresh.

Retail Display
American Girl

Store windows have long been a primary means of encouraging shoppers to enter the store. Centuries ago merchants would create elaborate scenes within the windows to stop passersby, particularly around Christmas time. Sprinkled throughout these elaborate scenes were typically some of the products that could be purchased in the store. As means of animating these windows became available, merchants began including little movements in the scenes, better stopping and holding the traffic passing by. This technique is still used by large retail establishments today.

American Girl Christmas window display '00

American Girl, now a division of Mattel, has created a cultural phenomenon around their dolls. When they decided to open their first store front named American Girl Place in Chicago, the Christmas windows had to live up to the over-the-top window displays that are a tradition along Chicago's famed Miracle Mile. They also had to live up to the cultural phenomenon status the dolls have achieved.

The Objectives
1) Hold the potential buyer's attention.
While most people glance at store front windows while Christmas shopping, that is usually all they do. Two techniques were used in the windows to hold people's attention: 1) one year the windows were packed with animated figures so that it took several minutes just to see everything in the windows; and 2) sequential animation was used – something happened that caused something else to happen. The show held the audience's attention because they wanted to see the outcome of the string of events.

2) Showcase as much product as possible.
Because American Girl is such a phenomenon, the window did not need to explain what the store was selling, it simply had to showcase the product. To help increase the amount of room within each of the relatively small windows, the sets were designed on a steep incline, effectively doubling the visual footprint of the scene.

3) The dolls had to be reusable each year.
The windows needed to be fiscally responsible. While theme parks and museums may be able to charge admission to see their shows, retail windows typically do not. That meant the armature design for each character had to fit entirely inside the figure, so that one year the doll could stand on an ice skating pond, and the next year it could sit in an oversized ornament. The result is a series of animated doll figures that can plug into whatever design American Girl creates each year.

An interview with American Girl designer, Shane McCall

Where do you get your inspiration?
You know, I've always been fascinated with broadway shows. For me, it's all in the theater set design. It just amazes me. The way the designers create and manipulate reality as well as the way they make things shift and move. It's absolutely fascinating. So philisophically, I reference the theatrics of theater. But you have to understand that as a designer, I draw from everything I can experience - video, film, music, books, magazines, movies - the world. I'm always thinking about new projects. Always looking for ideas. Always spinning off what I experience in other areas of my life, including my children. Fundamentally, I strongly believe you have to be creative in researching new ways to be creative.

What is it about animation that fascinates you?
Movement stops people, catches their eye and makes them notice what is actually happening. It makes them want to visually explore. If you go back in time, window displays usually had some kind of movement to grab people's attention. Most of today's windows have stationary displays, but even if the display had just a blinking light or a waving cardboard arm, it would create more interest. Animation has always worked and will continue to be effective. It's the visual psychology of human nature.

Your Christmas window displays for American Girl have been winning First Place Awards for the last few years. What part does animation play?
It's critical! It is an inherent part of what we design. Our windows are fantasy experiences for both children and adults. We design them to tell a story but not necessarily a sequential story. You never know where the window audience will start or how long they'll stay – much less what the range of ages will be. So it becomes a challenge to make mini-stories within a major story. That's where animation really helps create excitement. You can load surprises throughout the display that periodically unfold and develop. Hence burying and hiding eye-candy throughout the display.

Tell us about 2000's Christmas Window Display…specifically the design process.
Our big story idea was to translate an idea I got in the middle of the night. What would Chicago have looked like if the American Girl Collection Character Dolls had visited the city during their time periods, ranging from 1776 to 1994. And that was a big challenge – over a couple hundred years to illustrate and then to animate in only two windows. I know we wanted to really distort the visual reality. I wanted the building to have forced perspective. In fact, the whole display had forced perspective. We had 18" dolls next to 2" trees next to 10" boats next to 8" cars. Then we added the movement. We actually animated our dolls for the first time with subtle but realistic movement – waist bends, arms waving, clapping, etc. It was that movement that pulled all the static and lighting components together to create the magic. I knew we had an award winner when we had to wipe all those nose prints off the window each morning.

Retail Display
Jungle Jim's International Market

While themed environments and animatronic figures have become mainstays in toy stores, they are still relatively new to other retail environments. Jungle Jim's International Market is one of the pioneers incorporating animatronics into a non-toy retail environment. Located in Fairfield, Ohio, Jungle Jim's is a one-of-a-kind international food store selling food from just about every country on the planet. Jim Bonamino, the owner, wanted the store to match his personality…entertaining and eccentric.

On any given day, Jim may be found roller skating through the store playing shopping games or fishing for customers with twenty dollar bills from his office balcony, high above the store floor. To maintain this level of entertainment even when he is not around, Jim has incorporated themed environments, unusual props, and animatronic figures.

The Figures
General Mills Cereal Band
A trio of General Mills cereal characters sit high atop the dry goods wing of the store playing songs from the 50s and 60s. Trix the rabbit plays the keyboard, Lucky the Leprechaun sings and plays the guitar, and Honey Bee plays the bee hive drums.

Robin Hood
Based on the famous legend, this animatronic figure welcomes people to an international food wing of the store. He stands next to a huge tree (12-foot wide trunk) that is mounted above several of the aisles of the store. He sings and tells stories about his adventures. If visitors look up when they walk down the aisle beneath the tree, they can see some of the treasure about which he is singing.

The Objectives
1) Lengthen the experience.
Because Jungle Jim's is a source of many types of food that are not available in most stores, customers drive 2 and 3 hours to shop at the store. And while it can take a few hours to shop through the entire store, Jim wanted to offer a broader experience for his customers to make the trip an enjoyable day-long event. The animatronic character shows are placed at several locations throughout the store to provide a nice break from the shopping. Children also have fun trying to find the next show location.

2) Respect the brand's identity.
One of the criteria from the General Mills company was that the cereal band be created in such a way that it supported the identity already created by the company. The look, movements, and personality could not detract from what the audience expected from the characters made popular by the company's advertising campaigns. Working from General Mills-approved designs and colors, the figures had to be translated from the 2-dimensional images they had always been, into the 3-dimensional shapes of animatronic characters. The sculpts, textures, and movements were all compared to the established images of the figures. The result was a translation of the figures that people believed were the actual characters.

The General Mills Cereal Band entertains shoppers daily.

Science Centers
Taipei Astronomical Museum

While themed environments have long been used by museums and science centers to enhance their message, it is only recently that animatronics have really begun to be considered a viable medium for communicating the content. This recent explosion of animatronics in museums is due largely to the increased reliability and decreased maintenance requirements that the designers of animatronic figures have accomplished. Animatronics can now be used to tell stories, demonstrate processes, and interact directly with visitors.

The Taipei Astronomical Museum was looking for a way to convey how expansive space is, and what possibilities it holds for the future. The solution was a custom dark ride that took visitors on a journey through the cosmos. The experience included unique animatronics, an immersive environment, and a highly sophisticated ride system.

The Figures
Good aliens
Representing the possibilities of working with other species throughout the galaxy to improve life.

Bad aliens
Representing the dangers and cautions associated with the exploration of space.

Robots
Used when the focus of the experience was on new technologies and exploration, as opposed to the potential for contact with friendly or unfriendly aliens.

The Objectives
1) Quickly represent the pros and cons of exploring space.
One of the challenges of delivering a message in any situation where the audience is moving, such as in a queue or on a ride, is that the message needs to be delivered in a relatively short amount of time. If the audience does not "get it," they may not understand the rest of the message as it unfolds further into the experience. One technique used to help make the communication process more efficient is to use archetypes. These are basically classic configurations of characteristics most people can instantly recognize – the warrior, the villain, etc. By using archetypes of good and bad aliens, the attraction was able to quickly convey the story.

2) Keep the audience's attention.

Two techniques were employed to keep the audience's attention: a hidden camera in the figures and a water spray in a figure. A camera was hidden in the head of a robot animatronic in the queue area, and connected to a monitor that was part of the themeing. Audiences could then see themselves as the robot saw them. The water spray was part of an effect where the alien appears to be breaking out of a stasis tube. As the car passes by, the alien moves violently, sound effects are triggered, and water sprays at the audience as the alien appears to be breaking free.

3) Serviceability

The figures had to be easily serviced by the staff. Hidden access panels worked for all of the figures except one – the alien in the stasis tube. This figure was completely surrounded by a double wall cylinder with end caps. A track and dolly system was created that allowed the figure to slide out one end to access the valves and cylinders. The water pump and bubbler mechanism were located beneath the cylinder in a hidden cavity in the floor.

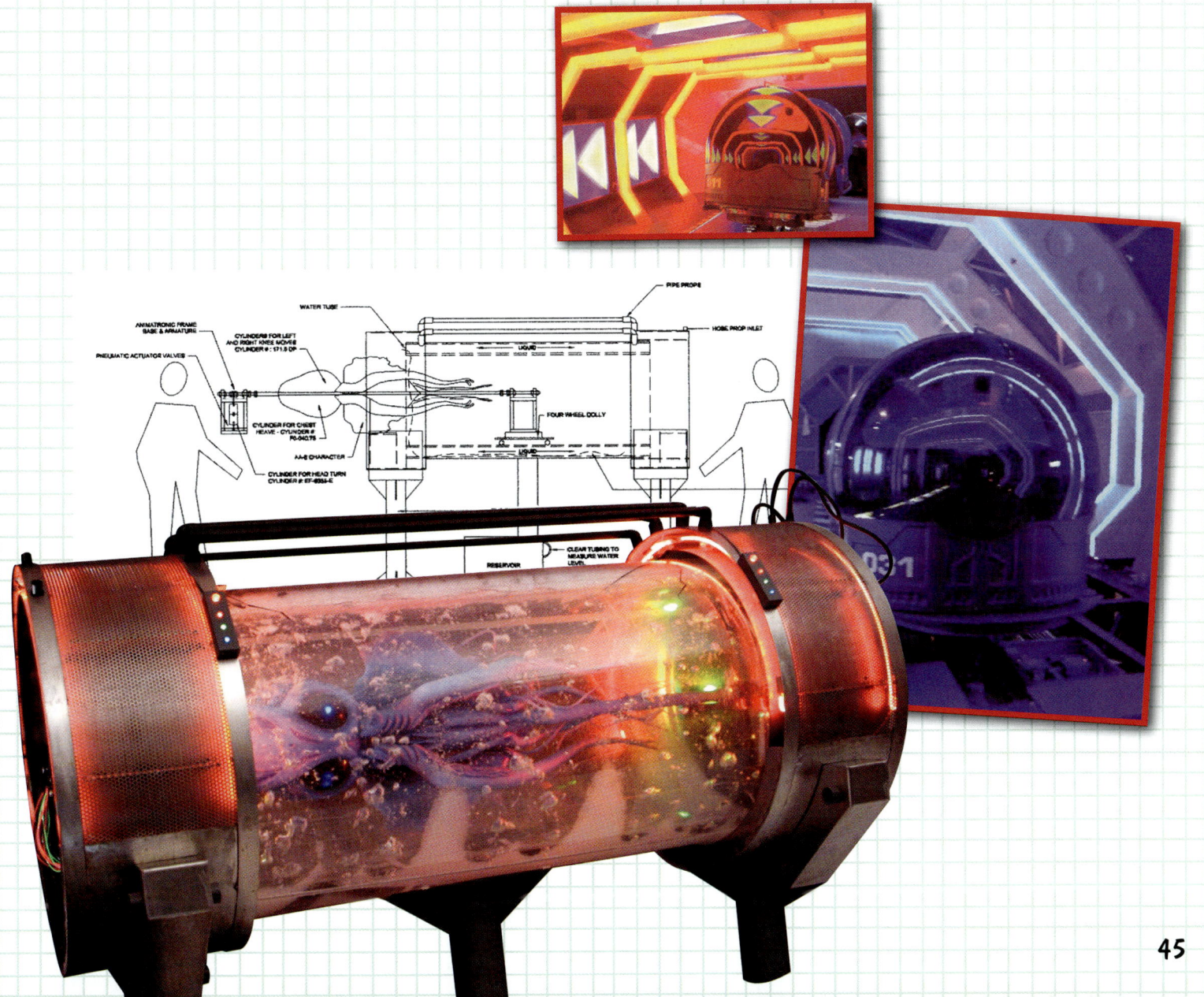

Science Centers
Health Royale

A major challenge for exhibit designers and producers is to create an unattended exhibit that does not feel *canned* or *pre-programmed*. In other words, they want to create an exhibit that appears to be responding directly to the visitor interacting with it, without having it operated by a live employee. Certainly there are several cause and effect type exhibits that can be created, but these tend to feel forced as there is usually only a few variables to adjust before the exhibit has been completely experienced.

The Avampato Science Center hosts one of the most interactive automated exhibits ever created. The game is based on the simple game of trivia tic tac toe – two competing players must correctly answer a question before they are awarded a square. Players choose a square by touching the corresponding square on their touchscreen. The skeleton host then asks a question of the 3-foot tall animatronic body part that occupies the chosen square. The player agrees or disagrees with the answer. If the player is correct, he or she wins the square. If they are incorrect, their opponent gets the square. Wisecracks and bantering back and forth help keep the game entertaining for everyone.

Nine characters and a host interact seamlessly with two players.

Speaking technically, 12 games with varying degrees of difficulty containing over 130 minutes of possible scripts (questions, answers, jokes, etc) are instantly accessed depending on which square is chosen in which game. Once accessed, 75 different character movements, 12 channels of audio, lighting cues, and special effects are instantly synchronized across 6 control systems so that the entire exhibit appears to be *real*.

The Figures
Skully the host
A 2-foot tall skeleton host dressed in a tuxedo, his personality is a take-off of Groucho Marx.

Queen Intestine
From across the pond, the pompous British personality has a problem controlling gastronomic activities. Her movements are all created with moving blobs of intestines.

Lips
A great big pair of lips. This character is reminiscent of Marilyn Monroe. The mouth move is almost the entire figure.

Mr. P
A giant bladder. This character is always in a bad mood. His eyes are half filled with yellow liquid.

Coach Heart
The physical fitness champion of the group. He is always lecturing the other parts on the importance of exercise.

Funny Bone
The smart-aleck of the group. She jumps up and down when she gets excited, causing her springy hair to bob all around.

Pelvis
The cool guy in the group. His powerful hip moves are reminiscent of the incomparable Elvis.

Slim Pick-It
A giant nose with a tendency to sneeze. His key movement is moving his hat up and down to create a variety of emotions and expressions.

The center square - Funny Bone.

Brain in a Jar
This character is surrounded by a double wall tube with bubbles floating in water contained between the tube walls giving the illusion that the character is submerged.

Mrs. Lung
The recently widowed wife of a long time smoker, she has a raspy voice and a nasty cough.

The Objectives
1) Easy to play.
The audience can instantly recognize the exhibit as a tic tac toe game, and so approaches it with the expectation that it will be as easy to play as tic tac toe. Touchscreen monitors are used for the player interface. Each touchscreen has an image of the large character tic tac toe board. Players select the desired square by touching it on the touchscreen. Taken squares have either an X or O in them.

The 13-foot tall exhibit has a couple of features to help both the players and the audience keep track of the game. Back lighting colors the boxes one of three colors: purple for not taken, red for taken by X, and blue for taken by O. Additionally, a small box pops up in the front of the square with either a red X or a blue O when a square is won.

2) Appearance of being a live show.
The designers wanted the entire show to operate as though these body parts were living actors playing the game with the contestants. This meant that the control system had to instantly translate the touching of a square on the touchscreen into a series of control signals to activate the control systems required to operate the exhibit.

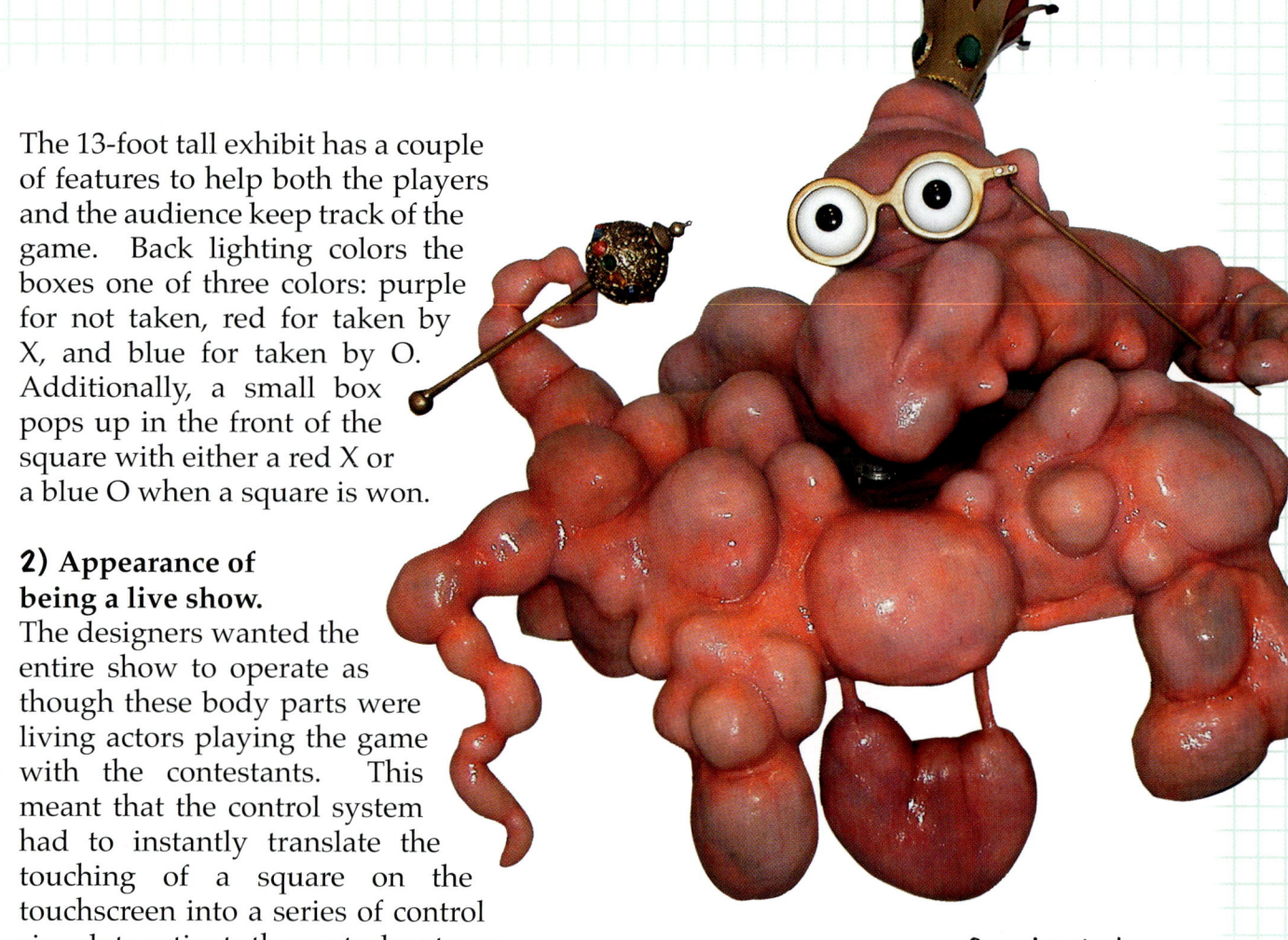

Queen Intestine has some problems controlling her gas.

Each player option was factored into the show. For example, if a player is taking too long to pick a square, a subroutine will run which causes the characters to act impatient and encourage the player to pick a square. The character movements, lighting, and special effects are programmed and controlled to hide the constant jumping between the 600 possible character scripts.

Ultimately, the audience cannot identify when the control system is jumping between scripts. The characters' movement maintain the appearance that they are alive and simply playing the game. The supporting effects have the appearance that they are being operated live on a stage.

Pelvis adds a well known personality along with some comical pelvic swings.

The sneezing Slim Pick-It incorporates a wiggling moustache to represent talking.

With her sexy voice, Lips adds yet another personality to the game.

Trailer-based Traveling Exhibit
M3 Marketing

One of the biggest obstacles when using animatronics as a communication medium, is that they are location based. In other words, someone has to travel to the animatronics figure or show if they are going to experience the figure. Some groups, however, have been able to overcome this limitation by installing their figures on semi-trailers that have been completely transformed into traveling exhibits. One of these organizations was M3 Marketing, a division of Aspen Marketing.

M3 Marketing designed a trailer-based traveling exhibit that highlighted the American Film Institute's 100 Years 100 Films campaign. The trailer featured costumes, props, scripts, and an assortment of other Hollywood artifacts from some of the films on their top 100 list. Alongside these artifacts were descriptions of the films and their significance in cinema history. LifeFormations created a figure that served as a transition between the environment in which the trailer was parked, and the magical world of Hollywood presented within the trailer.

World's oldest theater ticket taker greets guests.

The Figure
The World's Oldest Theater Ticket Taker had to be friendly yet authoritative, and could not invite comparisons to real movie stars. The goal was for the figure to establish credibility. The costume immediately identified the figure as a theater ticket taker – someone who would be knowledgeable about films. The facial features were an exaggerated caricature of an elderly butler or chauffer that did not resemble any popular movie stars. The expression was entertaining, yet the age subtly established authority and encouraged respect.

The Objectives
The figure served as a transition between the outside world and the exhibits within the trailer. As such, it had to accomplish 3 objectives:

1) Frame the experience.
The people entering this exhibit had just stepped into it from a variety of uncontrolled environments such as grocery store parking lots, city parks, and school playgrounds. The figure's most important objective was to quickly block out everything going on outside the vehicle, and then spark audience interest about great films of the past century. The Ticket Taker figure was able to create this transition by delivering key movie lines and trivia relating to the films that would help the audience access their own experiences related to the movies.

With these experiences fresh in the visitors' minds, they were able to better personalize the content, tying it to their own memories or knowledge.

2) Provide a quick orientation.
This was not an exhibit where people could simply roam around killing time until they got the lay of the land and were ready to consume the content. This was a tight space built along a central aisle down the center of the truck. There was a long line that kept steady pressure on everyone to keep moving forward. If a visitor wanted to go back and see something they passed by too quickly at the beginning, he or she had to go wait in line again. The Ticket Taker figure inserted short descriptions of the exhibit, and where featured items could be seen. These directions could be heard not only by visitors standing at the entrance to the exhibit, but also by many of those waiting in line. When they actually entered the exhibit, visitors already knew where to look for many of the artifacts.

3) Establish a brisk pace.
Rain or shine, if someone wanted to see the exhibit, they had to stand in the cue area outside the trailer. To keep people from becoming bored or discouraged with the wait, the audiences experiencing the exhibit had to keep a relatively steady pace forward through the exhibit. The short, excited speaking style of the Ticket Taker helped maintain an energized feeling throughout the entire trailer, which kept people moving relatively quickly.

Where are they now?

The World's Oldest Ticket Taker has enjoyed 2 more incarnations since the 100 Years 100 Films tour ended. He next became the World's Oldest Sportscaster for an ESPN tour, and most recently underwent a head transplant and became George Blaha, voice of the Detroit Pistons.

George Blaha is actually the ticket taker revamped.

Stage Show
The Big Yummy

The audience with the shortest attention span probably belongs to elementary school students on a field trip. Creating an exhibit that successfully communicates something as complicated as how food gets from the farmer's field to the kitchen table can be something of a tall order. COSI Columbus was given just such a challenge when they received a grant to help create an exhibit about agriculture.

When the agriculture exhibit came up, they decided to turn a lunchroom into an old vaudeville dinner theater style show. Students are invited to eat their lunch during a 30-minute talent show where the food is the star and agriculture is the theme. The actors sing and dance about the role agriculture plays in everyone's lives. At the end of the show, the host invites the crowd to select the winner of the prestigious *Big Yummy* award.

The Figures

Leche, the host
A 4-foot tall milk carton on a 20-foot long track, Leche is able to enter from the rear of the stage, exit stage left, and stop anywhere along the way. He was made largely of fabric to allow considerable stretching.

Corn Cob Bob and Butter, the ventriloquist act
The facial features of the corn cob figure floating above the face, creating a very stylized look of 2-D animation but on a 3-D figure. The butter figure has a huge drop jaw similar to old ventriloquist dummies, helping to push the stylized design even further.

Tofu, the tap dancer
Suspended from behind so she can pop through the curtain and appear to be floating. This allows her legs to kick around freely just above the stage floor.

Tomato, the dare devil
Slides back into the canon to be fired across the room. A smashed tomato figure was created and installed on the opposite wall, with just legs wiggling back and forth.

Beans, the acrobats
Bouncing up and down on a stretchable cloth, allowing them to look like they are really jumping on the drum head.

Free animation

Free animation is used to describe a movement in a figure that is not directly driven, but rather is the result of other movement within the figure. For example, the Bean characters in the Big Yummy show had teeth mounted to springs and a track. When the figure jumped up and own, the inertia of the teeth caused them to bounce up and down without an actuator. It is actually a misnomer to call it free animation, as it takes about the same time to fabricate these types of movement as it does a cylinder driven movement.

Their teeth were mounted to springs to achieve free animation (see sidebar: Free Animation).

Leftover, the blues singer
A big blob of different colors and textures, Leftover sings the blues because nobody likes him.

Hardboiled Egg, the heckler
Actually sits in the audience. The top of him raises up and down to make his mouth move.

The Objectives
1) Attract their attention.
Certainly this is an objective of any exhibit or attraction, but with elementary school students, it is particularly difficult to accomplish. The characters have to be something they haven't seen before, and they have to be believable. This situation creates something in visitors we call *hindsight expectations*. This occurs when an audience does not have any formed expectations before seeing something, but can immediately critique why something did or did not meet their expectations after they see it. This happens when someone sees something like a Dragon, an alien, or in this case, talking food.

For the *Big Yummy* characters, hindsight expectations were both a blessing and a challenge. On one hand, nobody has seen a daredevil tomato sitting in a canon before, so the audience does not have anything against which to compare the figure. Whatever the character looks like, it should be accepted by them as normal. On the other hand, because there is no existing benchmark, believability becomes very subjective. Although the audience may not have seen other stunt daredevil tomato figures, they have seen other daredevils, and they have seen other tomatoes. Items like a tomato's color, texture, and movement, as well as a daredevil's voice and personality must be at least loosely followed to create the suspension of disbelief for the audience (see sidebar: Suspension of Disbelief).

Suspension of disbelief

Suspension of disbelief is a willingness of the audience to forget that they are merely watching a show, and accept the reality of the show as their own reality. This is the same phenomenon that makes watching a movie enjoyable – particularly science fiction and fantasy films. The audience is willing to ignore production limitations and accept what is shown without questioning whether or not it is real or even possible.

When the finished project is able to withstand hindsight expectations, and allow the audience to create and maintain their suspension of disbelief, the audience is sucked into the show and the message can be delivered.

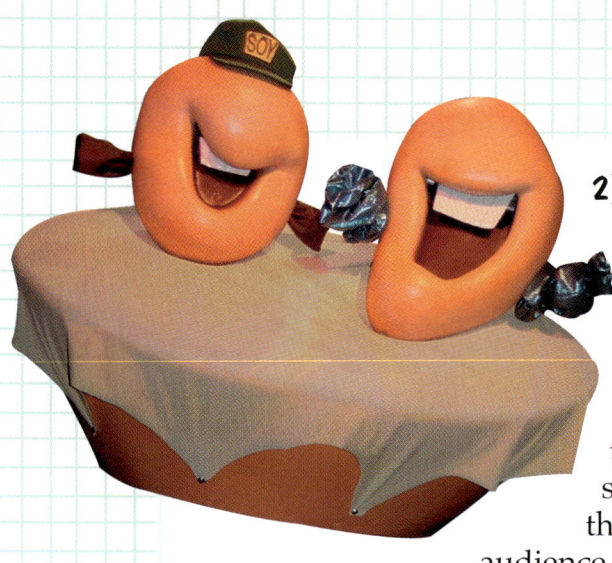

2) Hold their attention.

Once the audience is sucked into the show, their attention must be held for the duration of the show. In the exhibit world, this is called holding power. Is the exhibit able to hold the attention of the visitor long enough to deliver the intended message or provide the intended experience? Given the length of this show – 30 minutes – there were several attention holding techniques used. One of the key audience holding techniques is *the reveal*. The audience is never quite sure where the next character will appear. Sometimes they enter from the side of the stage. Sometimes they rise up through the floor. Sometimes they poke through the curtain. The show cannot afford to become predictable or it will not be able to hold the audience's attention.

Another holding technique used is bouncing the audience's attention between characters. Just like a human actor, the characters can only hold an audience's attention for so long. Generally, the more movement a figure has, the longer it can hold the audience's attention. And by combining figures, a Gestalt effect is created. The holding time of several characters bantering back and forth is longer than the sum of each character's individual holding time.

The law of numbers

The more figures involved in the show and the more times they pass the audience's attention back and forth, the longer the audience will stay interested. The Big Yummy ran about 30 minutes long, and had 10 characters. Each character was limited to 2 minutes on stage at a time, but usually it was even shorter.

For *The Big Yummy* there are at least three or four characters available to banter back and forth at any time. Obviously the host anchors the show, and is able to talk with the characters as they enter and exit the stage. Some of the actors are part of a team, such as the ventriloquist act and the bouncing beans. The Heckling Egg figure blurts out insults from the back of the theater and is always available to jump in where the show may need a little help keeping the audience's attention.

Leftovers sings the blues for one of the acts.

Get the audience involved

At the close of the show, the audience is asked to vote for their favorite act by clapping for one of the choices. A noise volume sensor detects which figure received the loudest clapping and plays the appropriate ending. A default choice is programmed into the show in case there are not enough people for the sensor to detect.

Wippalaffalux measures crowd response.

Maquettes

Maquettes are small sculpts of the larger figures. They are typically created on a scale of 1 - 2 inches per foot, and are created to be the primary reference for the character throughout the process. The proportions guide the sculpting process, the overall dimensions allow the design and fabrication departments to ensure the final character will hold the animatronic components, and the maquette's finish guides the art finishing.

Maquettes are typically created for unique characters, such as the one depicted here. This is Plunk, created by LifeFormations under the art direction of Allen Boerger of COSI Studio. More traditional figures, such as humans or animals, have enough existing photographic reference available that maquettes may not be necessary.

Research
Ken Feingold

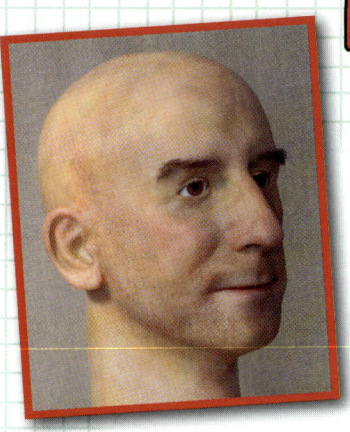

There have been a small number of studies that examine the potential interaction between humans and animatronic figures. One of the authors of this book examined the feasibility of a voice-activated exhibit that enabled visitors to ask Thomas Edison questions about many of his inventions. While the interface worked well, additional research was needed on the artificial intelligence aspect so that the system could better interact beyond a few simple key words.

Ken Feingold has recently created a series of exhibits that experiment with audience response to talking animatronic heads. The heads discuss philosophical questions through direct conversations with each other. In an almost stream-of-consciousness manner, the heads banter back and forth, picking up key words in what one of the other heads had just said. These key words may then either continue along the same conversation path, or may take a different direction, creating an entirely new meaning.

The Objectives
1) Have the heads be self-programming.
Because the heads are being controlled by an artificial intelligence-based system, it is impossible to pre-program them. The system is literally creating a new show every time. The solution to this is to use a voice-activated circuit that translates the audio signal created by the computer into a signal pulse that triggers the valves for the mouth moves. Because the computer generates a very consistent audio signal, it is possible to adjust the sensitivity of the voice-activated circuit to very accurately simulate proper mouth moves.

2) Keep the audience focused on the content.
To help keep the audience's attention focused on the content, the heads do not have hair or a body. They are mounted to a simple metal stand, with the bottom of the silicone being cleanly cut to give it a finished look.

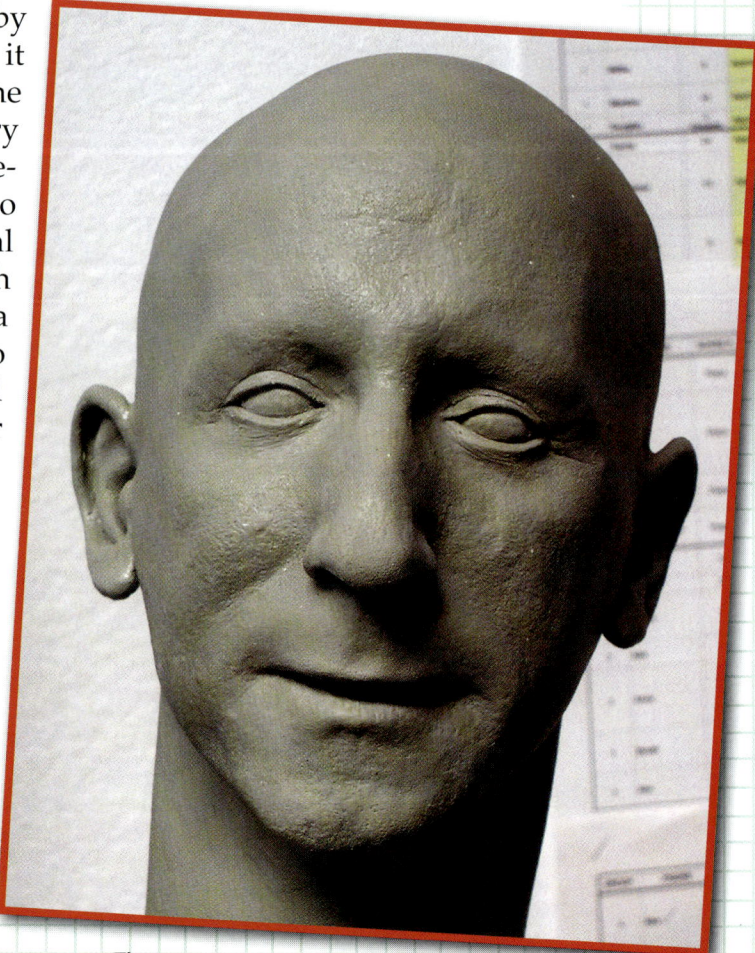

The heads are based on a lifecast of Ken's face.

Tradeshow
Rubbermaid

Fred the Fridge showing why he likes leftovers stored in Rubbermaid containers.

Rubbermaid needed a way to demonstrate how well its products worked. The solution was to create a refrigerator with two sides. One side showed what a refrigerator looks like if Rubbermaid products are not used. The other side showed what a refrigerator looks like if Rubbermaid products were used. The refrigerator has a deep voice and a loveable personality. He talks about how bad a refrigerator can be abused without Rubbermaid products, and how much more useable it is if Rubbermaid products are used.

The Figure
The refrigerator
Using the interior of a real refrigerator, this character was created on a base that allowed it to be simply rolled in and out of a crate. Both doors opened on cue, the face was animated and the eyes lit up when he got very excited.

Refrigerator contents
Mysterious things can occur when food is left unprotected in the refrigerator. These include a gremlin arm in the pizza box, a shaking can of beans, and a questionable box of leftovers.

The Objectives
1) Don't show the competition.
Rubbermaid needed to show how bad things could get in a refrigerator if their products were not used. They did not, however, want to show their competition's products in their booth. Instead, a series of generic boxes were used, along with food (artificial) sitting on the shelf.

2) Use humor.
One of the goals was to include humor in the show. The scripts were written to make fun of the food not in Rubbermaid containers, not of customers who did not use Rubbermaid. Additionally, the food on the non-Rubbermaid side took on its own personality, as described above. This created a sort of battle that people put their refrigerator through if they do not use Rubbermaid products.

Tradeshow
GenFlex

While animatronic technology can be used to bring products to life for tradeshow booths, there are times when animating the product is not the best choice. This is particularly true when the product's appearance is very similar to the competition's product. As tradeshow attendees return to their offices and try to remember their conversations at the show, it can be very easy to juxtapose one company's exhibit with another company's name. The animatronic figure should work to reduce this risk, not contribute to it.

GenFlex is a company that creates roofing materials for industrial buildings, among other items. These products are limited largely to rolls and buckets of various roofing products, as are those of their competition. If the rolls and buckets had simply been animated, the show may not have been identified with the Genflex name. Instead, an animated show was created with two animatronic buildings. One has a GenFlex roof, and one does not. They engage in several conversations about the importance of a good roof, and the resulting problems if a building does not have one.

Elvis IS the building at a Vegas tradeshow.

The Figures
Eddie
The building with the non-GenFlex roof. He is a younger building, not yet aware of the importance of proper building maintenance. He turns, hops up and down, blinks his eyes, opens his mouth, and has eyes that light up when he gets really upset about his tenants all moving out due to the leaky roof.

Hi-Rise Bill
The building with a GenFlex roof. He is the older, wiser building that tries to show Eddie the ropes of being a successful building. Bill's occupancy is always at capacity, and his tenants are always happy. The entire top half of Bill can rise up and lean in all directions. He can also open his mouth, turn side to side, and blink his eyes.

The Challenge
1) Be continually updated for use at future shows.
The characters were originally introduced as a pair of buildings bantering back and forth against a cityscape background. For the following year's tradeshows, a game show set was created with the host appearing on a video screen that was synchronized to the animatronic figures. Eddie and Bill were challenged with several questions about what makes a good roof. GenFlex's final tradeshow featuring the building theme was in Las Vegas, where Bill appeared solo as an Elvis impersonator. He sang Elvis-style songs with roofing themes.

Hi-Rise Bill and Eddie comparing their roofs at a tradeshow.

59

Tradeshow
Honeywell

As discussed earlier in this book, tradeshows are an incredibly difficult environment in which to compete for people's attention. This is certainly the case when your product sounds too good to be true. Honeywell's commercial HVAC division had just such a problem. They had a service plan in which they would come into an institution such as a hospital or university and completely upgrade the HVAC systems to more efficient, better responding systems. Their payment would then be a percentage of the savings the institution realized with the new equipment in place. Honeywell made money while the institution saved money. A true win/win situation.

But how could they make people stop and listen in the tradeshow climate of outrageous claims and too-good-to-be true offers? A series of figures were created that inhabited a school classroom, a hospital operating room, and a university president's office. They told the Honeywell story and sales literally increased fourfold.

The Shows
School
The chalkboard came to life as a video element that realized how much money the school was losing. The stone bust played the role of a crotchety founder of the school whose statue has come to life to express his disappointment in the way money is being wasted on the low efficiency utility systems. The computer monitor played the role of a know-it-all who was only too happy to share his knowledge about how Honeywell could help the school save money.

School Show

University
Similar to the School show, the University show replaced the blackboard with a university president too overwhelmed with financial crises to do much of anything except moan. This show also introduced an animated HVAC vent on the back wall to tell his own story of how bad the situation had gotten with his system.

University Show

Hospital
An operating room hosts this group. The lamp speaks on behalf of the patients and employees that have to live with a run down system. The vent explains how bad everything is, and the X-ray viewer calls on a variety of famous personalities to explain how Honeywell can help.

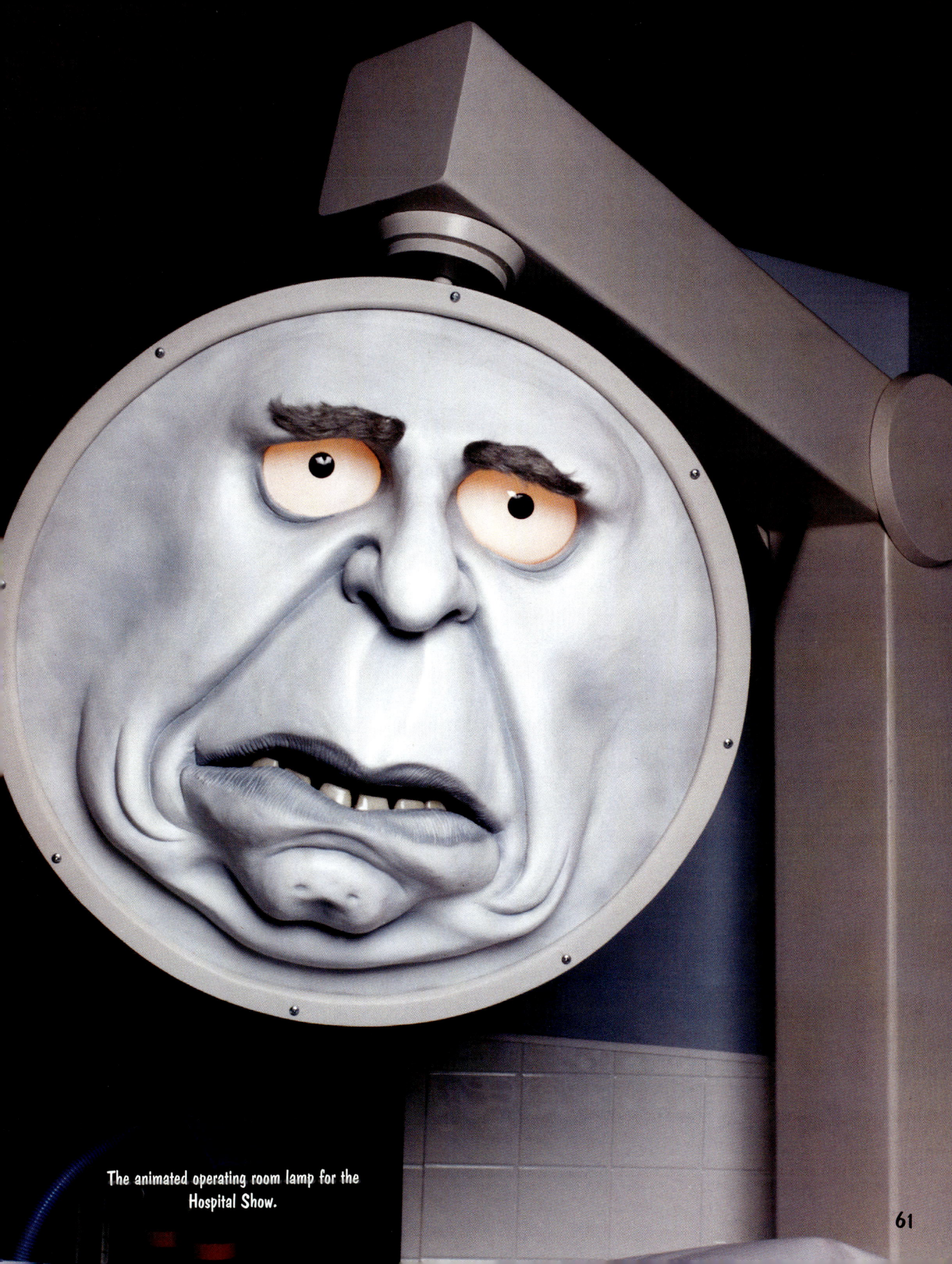

The animated operating room lamp for the Hospital Show.

The Objectives
1) Keep the audience's attention until the entire message is delivered.
Two techniques helped keep the audience's attention long enough for the fairly complex message to be delivered: the conflict and the reveal. The conflict was created by forcing extreme personalities to deal with each other in the show. These conflicting personalities waged a battle of wits that compelled the audience to stay until they found out who won.

The reveals were created by characters joining into the conflict one by one as the show progressed. Prior to their joining into the show, they appeared to be inanimate items – a statue, back of a computer monitor, lamp, etc. Just when audience members may consider moving on, a new character comes to life and keeps their attention.

2) Create a show with which the audience can identify.
It is one thing to create a booth or show that can stop an audience and hold their attention for a presentation. It is a whole different scenario to create a booth that touches the audience personally, allowing them to put themselves into the message. Honeywell wanted to do more than just create a show that would stop people long enough for the salespeople to catch them. They wanted to create a show that proved to the audience that Honeywell understood their situation. They wanted to make sure the audience would not dismiss the message as they might with other vendors, but would instead cause people to wait in lines to talk to salespeople.

The show was a metaphor for the drama played out in institutions every day. Each character was designed to reflect a real person in that drama. The busts and hospital lamp were designed to be the customers and employees complaining about a situation. The vents were designed to be the impending voice of doom from the maintenance department. And the computer and X-ray were knights in shining armor, bringing forth the solution to everyone's problems. By allowing the audience to substitute their own identity into the realistic situation, the solution became real.

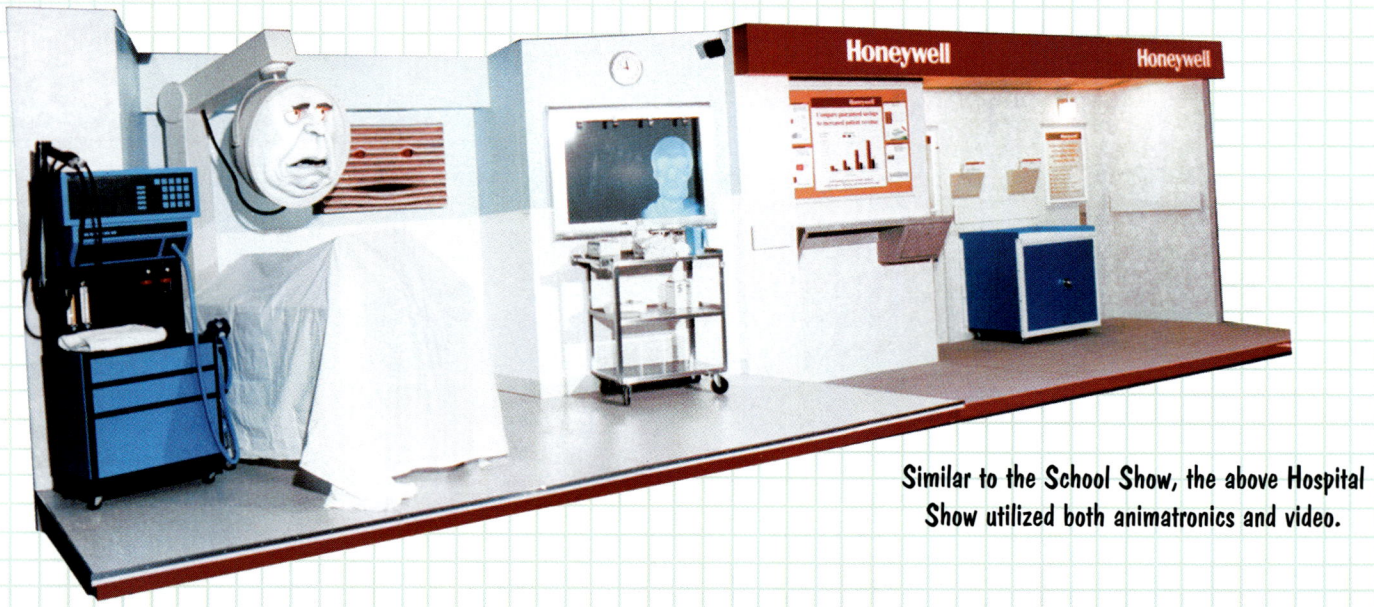

Similar to the School Show, the above Hospital Show utilized both animatronics and video.

Several other Honeywell characters have been created over the years, from animated money to the "World's Oldest Contractor," the Guru.

Tradeshow
Vacuflo of Ohio

In some ways, fair and home show exhibits are not unlike tradeshow or museum exhibits. That is, they are designed with the intention of either selling a product or communicating a concept.

In other ways product fairs and home show exhibits are very different. While a tradeshow or museum typically attracts a visitor that has an interest in what the museum or trade show features, a fair attracts visitors who may not yet realize they are interested in what a booth has to show them. Additionally, fairs encourage a more casual atmosphere than a museum or tradeshow. As a result, visitors tend to be more comfortable touching exhibit components – sometimes aggressively.

Vacuflo of Ohio sells and installs central vacuum cleaners. One of their primary customer groups is the people who wander the home and garden shows on the weekend. Some of these people are actively looking to improve their homes, others are just getting ideas for the future, and still others are just filling an afternoon. Vacuflo of Ohio owner Tom Dowd wants to stop them all.

Selected Figures
Benjamin Franklin
Marvels at the invention of Vacuflo and tells audiences about his own inventions.

Dr. Baktylife
Sings for the audience and also tells them how clean Vacuflo keeps even the house of a rotting corpse.

Madame Vacuuma
With her amazing crystal ball, she looks back to the turn of the century techniques of house cleaning and coaxes the audience to get into 21st century vacuuming with a VacuFlo System.

Old Man and Wife Porch Scene
This pair split their time between bickering about the old days of cleaning and praising the "new fangled" VacuFlo System.

The Duck
Tells the audience to treat themselves to a VacuFlo while also offering them ice cream.

Year after year the creative characters at the Vacuflo of Ohio booth bring in countless awards and aisle-jamming crowds at home shows.

The Objectives

1) Cost effective.

Tradeshow booths use magicians, impersonators, remote controlled robots and a variety of other *hooks* to get people into their booth. Each of these requires a live person that charges a day rate plus expenses. Tom averaged his annual expenses to hire these entertainers, cut it in half, and used that for his animatronic figure budget. The result was increased booth traffic on a decreased budget. Set-up time increased slightly, but he also never had to deal with talent no-shows or sick days.

Another problem Tom was having with his talent was their habit of pulling from a list of popular shows or routines that audiences had seen before. Audiences would stop, but then quickly move on once they realized they had seen the material before. By using original animatronic shows, the audience was held long enough for the salespeople to reach them.

2) They have to create marketing buzz.

It is difficult to create a public relations or marketing frenzy around central vacuum cleaners themselves. Tom uses the characters in his booth to create the buzz. He created an entire campaign around his Benjamin Franklin figure by advertising that the famous inventor was coming to check out the new Vacuflo system. At another show, he created an advertising campaign around a zombie character whose house only Vacuflo could keep clean. By combining the entertaining figures with the Vacuflo brand, Tom was able to create a memorable experience that stuck in people's minds.

Fairs - Moulton Gas

Similar to home shows, fairs offer a variety of products to visitors which they may not necessarily be in the market for at that time. Moulton Gas wanted a figure that would both attract people to their booth, and then entertain children while sales representatives talked with their parents. The animated Moulton Gas tank had a message that combined the benefits of using Moulton Gas with a strong safety message for children.

The opera singer belts out heart (and ear!) wrenching melodies about the joys of house cleaning with a Vacuflo.

From Tradeshow to Showroom
Midmark

One of the assumptions of most tradeshow exhibitors is that the people walking the show should have some interest in what the exhibitor is exhibiting. Based on this premise, one could hope that no matter how conservative or utilitarian their product, people would stop and look at it. And that would work, if other exhibitors did not employ non-product related, attention-getting tactics. So what is a conservative company with a utilitarian product left to do? Make their product more attention grabbing.

Midmark creates medical and dental products, such as sterilizers, medical cabinets, and examination chairs. They wanted a way to pull the tradeshow crowd into their booth. Having seen animated characters at other venues, they decided to try it for themselves... cautiously at first. They tried out one character at a show. When it was a success, they added a second character to showcase two products while the two bantered back and forth. Finally, a third figure was added when the exhibit moved permanently to their showroom.

The Figures
Erol
A sterilizer for medical instruments. Erol had a very dry personality. He was essentially a face on the front of a real sterilizer cabinet. The sterilizer cabinet was animated to turn, nod, open its door, and trigger the proper lights on the front control panel.

Lola
A medical examination chair, Lola had a sultry voice and a friendly personality. Her headrest was actually an animated face, and her programming included both the face and all of the functions of the chair as well.

Casey
Casey was a piece of modular casework. He was the confused one in the group, regularly asking for clarification on whatever the other two were discussing. His face was the entire front of the cabinet.

The Objectives
1) Take advantage of existing components and functions.
Obviously Midmark wanted to save money wherever it could. One of the ways this was accomplished was by using their actual products as much as possible. They provided the outside cabinet of the sterilizer so that only a new front face needed to be created. When the second figure was added, only a couple of moves in the face needed to be animated, because the entire chair had several movements built in to facilitate the medical examination process. The control system simply tied into these existing functions.

Lola the Examination Chair

2) Create an incentive for visitors.
Midmark is located in a remote part of the state of Ohio. They know their showroom can demonstrate their products better than their brochures and other marketing materials, so they needed to create incentives for people to take the time to visit their facility. One of those incentives is a very dynamic showroom. The first stop in the showroom is a medical examination room populated with the three figures. They tell the story of Midmark products themselves.

3) Change shows based on the audiences.
Given the diverse audiences that attend the various tradeshows Midmark attends, their salespeople needed a way to play different shows simply. The control system was set up with multiple playlists, each applying to a different audience. Through a simple PC interface, the salespeople could load the appropriate show in a matter of a seconds. The control system would then either wait for an input from a pushbutton or play on a timed schedule, depending on which option was loaded.

When the figures were installed in the Midmark showroom, two push buttons were installed. The salespeople push one button to play a greeting to the showroom and another button to play a farewell show.

Both Erol and Lola utilized many pieces from the actual products they represented.

Things to Consider

The following pages present some general ideas to consider when designing an exhibit or attraction that will include animatronic figures. While they are certainly not inclusive of everything that must be considered, they do cover some of the general decisions and processes that are part of every animatronic character.

There are three main systems involved with an animatronic figure: the animatronic itself, the air supply, and the control system. While the following pages focus primarily on the animatronic itself, the diagram to the right shows how the animatronic interfaces with the related systems.

Animatronic character
The animatronic is a combination of artistic and mechanical components working together to create a moving character.

Compressor or pump
If the character is pneumatic, an air compressor and dryer provide a clean compressed air supply to operate the character. If the character is hydraulic, a hydraulic pump and filter provide a clean fluid supply to operate the character. If the character is electric, there is simply a power supply.

Control system
The control system may be dedicated exclusively to the animatronic, or it may operate an entire show. Even if it is dedicated to the animatronic, the control system must interface somehow with its environment – either through push buttons, timers, or communication with another control system.

Animatronic Systems

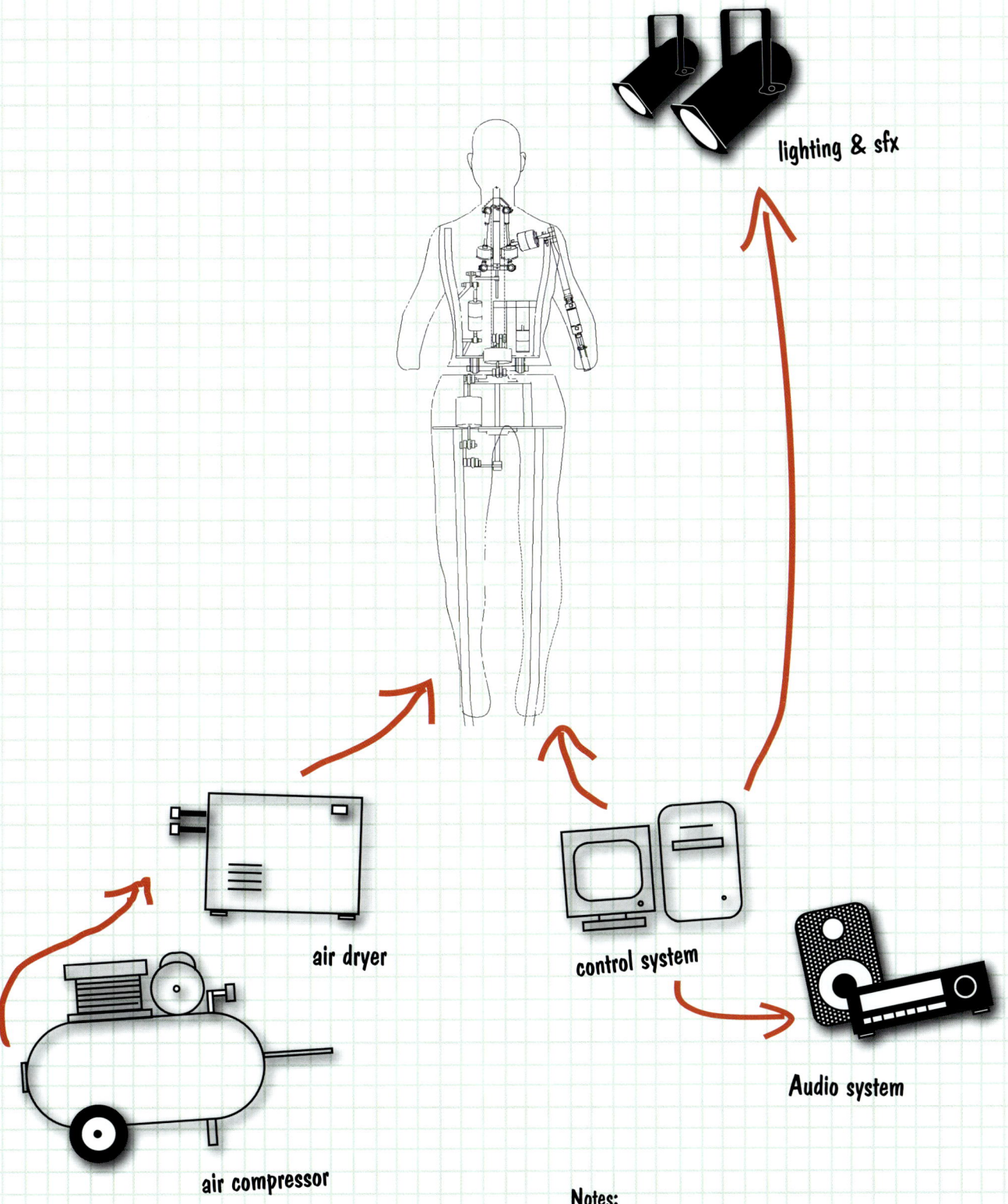

lighting & sfx

air dryer

control system

Audio system

air compressor

Notes:
- many times speakers are located in or very near the character to make the audio sound more believable.
- control systems range from PC's to eprom devices.

Things to Consider
Sculpting a Likeness

Few jobs challenge or even frustrate a sculptor more than sculpting a portrait figure. To some, sculpting a block of clay to resemble a person's face/head may seem to be a relatively straightforward process…take a few measurements, reference a few photographs and viola you have a likeness. Not so. Likenesses require every square millimeter to be in the exact relationship it was on the real person or the likeness does not work.

And it can get tougher than that. Even when the relationship of every facet of the face is correct, preconceived notions of personality and expression can still lead people to question the likeness. We have experienced this first hand when we created lifecasts that the person who was cast later denied was them. They were either unprepared to see the reverse image of what they typically see (remember, you are used to seeing yourself in the mirror, which shows you the reverse of what those looking at you see); or they were not happy with the expression they had when being cast.

Even when the group of people involved with the project are happy with the likeness, others may not be. Probably the most famous venue to experience this phenomenon is Madame Tussauds Wax Museum. Plant yourself close to a celebrity likeness and listen to the various reactions people have. They will range from "exact match" to "not even close." While some of their likenesses are certainly stronger than others, it's not necessarily their fault. People just have different, often mythologized images of celebrities in their minds.

Consider Elvis Presley. He's as tough as they come to re-create. Most people have their own personal vision of Elvis. Some have an older, heavier Elvis in mind. Others have a movie Elvis look in mind. Still others think of Elvis as he first appeared on the Ed Sullivan Show. Add to that the fact that people often experience certain emotions when they see Elvis, and it gets a little scary. Creating a figure that matches every possible vision of Elvis while generating the expected emotions is nearly impossible.

And so it is with many famous people. A $1/32^{nd}$ of an inch can throw off the whole likeness. Take a Halloween mask and manipulate the surfaces with your fingers and see how the overall character look changes. The mask may still be recognizable, but it's not realistic. And that's what the audience will expect…realism.

Does all this mean you should stay away from likenesses? Absolutely not. A likeness allows the audience to experience the figure in three dimensions. They can walk around it…touch it…interact with it. This can be a far more powerful experience than simply looking at a photograph or reading a description.

Pose, costume and expression must all be considered when creating a likeness, as with Lillian Gish, created for Bowling Green State Unversity's Gish Theater.

So what do you do?

Stage the experience as though the audience just interrupted your subject from whatever it is he or she would normally be doing.

A portrait figure is about more than just what the figure's face looked like. It's also about what the person did and how they did it. One of the worst things a designer can do is to pull a portrait figure out of his or her context and put him or her front and center on a stage. The audience is left with nothing to judge about the person except the likeness.

Here are a few elements to consider:

1) Have the pose and gesture of the person reflect a common activity he or she would have been doing: working at a workbench, leaning against a doorway, or something else just as natural.

2) Frame the figure with supporting elements. These are items that help tell the story. A prop in the hand or a piece of furniture around the figure can immediately help the figure convey the details of his or her story.

3) Keep the expression of the face consistent with audience expectations. If the person was always happy, make sure there is a hint of a smile on the figure. If they were never happy, make sure you don't try to force a smile into the likeness…the audience will not accept it.

Norman Rockwell figure with careful consideration taken in capturing one of his common poses.

Costume authenticity can be a very important factor in capturing likenesses, as with this Satchel Paige figure for the Negro Leagues Basball Museum.

Typically when capturing a likeness, a very high level of detail is demanded as with this animated Thomas Edison. Age marks, beard stubble and hand-poked hair are all included.

ESPN's Lou Gehrig was created to allow fans to experience his famous speech face-to-face. Footage of the event was researched to ensure that the proper pose, moves and expression were chosen.

Things to Consider
The Continuum of Animatronic Moves

An animatronic move is simply an action the character can perform. For example, an eye blink, a wrist turn, a head turn to the right, and a head turn to the left, are all common examples of character moves. Animatronic characters can have as few as one move (such as a mouth) or as many 40 or more movements. Movements are sometimes referred to as degrees of freedom.

Animatronic movements are typically not very precise when compared to industrial robots. The industrial types measure precision in thousandths of an inch. What their movements look like is not really a factor -- just their accuracy in placement. Animatronic characters are designed to move with natural, human/animal like action -- where performance is actually measured in believability and audience appeal.

Actuation Technologies
There are three types of technologies that animatronic movements use: pneumatic, electrical, and hydraulic. Each has its strengths and weaknesses, and careful consideration of all three is necessary to match the goal of the project to the performance of the movement technology.

For most animatronic applications, pneumatic movement is the best solution. Pneumatic movement simply means that the character movements are a function of air cylinders causing the action. Pneumatic activation is very reliable - it's rated in the millions of cycles. That may sound like an exorbitant number, but think about a character talking all day long, every day of the year, for many years. If it ran a one minute show every five minutes over the course of a 12 hour day, that is about 8,500 open/close movements a day, or 3 million a year.

Pneumatic movement is also relatively inexpensive, as compared to something like a hydraulic system. And pneumatic movement is quiet in operation, because it is simply air being pushed through a tube. It does, however, require that an air compressor be installed in the facility. While there are many different types of air compressors - loud, quiet, big, small - all require some sort of maintenance on a weekly basis.

There are animatronic characters that use electric motors, or servos. Electrically activated characters are typically very simple animations like those found in Christmas display windows. Servo technology has just barely begun to overcome past problems of the relatively short life span of its parts. While they work great for applications such as model planes, where the servo may only be fired once a minute during a one hour flight each week, they could not hold up to the rigors of traditional animation applications. They are also very noisy, as the gears turn to actuate the movement. While they are relatively inexpensive, the cost of replacing them often has relegated them to special applications only.

Hydraulic movement is typically reserved for very large figures such as life-size dinosaurs, or figures with very sophisticated movement where quick speed is required and/or space is limited. Hydraulics incorporates a liquid as a medium to activate character movement. Typically this medium is oil and operates at a much higher pressure -- usually at 400-600 pounds per square inch compared to 80-100 for air. Because of this higher pressure of activation, cylinder size and weight can be reduced. A negative quality of hydraulics is that it is not as spongy as air and can look very stiff and mechanical. Hydraulic technology also tends to be very expensive. And finally, when a hydraulic line blows, oil is sprayed everywhere, as opposed to a pneumatic move, which would only blow air everywhere.

Movement Control

The simplest and least expensive type of actuation is called a digital move. The analogy of a digital move is a standard toggle light switch - it is either on or off. For example, a digital head nod is either up (on) or down (off) or moving somewhere along its travel stroke to either extreme. It has no ability to stop in between the two extremes. And it has no ability to change speed because the speed is preset by adjusting individual air flow controls placed in the air hoses. Changing the speed of the move requires accessing the figure and manually adjusting the flow rate. Many animatronic characters are built with all digitally controlled movements, especially non-human ones.

An analog move has infinite control over both the speed of the move and where the move stops along its stroke. The analogy for this movement would be a light dimmer switch - you can control both the speed of the dimming as well as the ability to park the brightness anywhere in a range from light to dark. There is no need to manually adjust the flow rate inside the figure; it is all taken care of with the control system. This superior control creates superior looking movements when compared to digital movements, but the equipment to create an analog movement is more complex and more expensive than the equipment needed to create a digital movement. Therefore, it is not unusual for a lifelike character to have a combination of analog and digital movements to achieve the best of both worlds: overall movement "look" and reasonable price.

A pseudo-analog movement is a third option for controlling pneumatic movements. It really is a digital-controlled movement with a specific valve configuration that almost gives the look and control of an analog movement, but does not require additional care in programming.

One last element of control technology that is occasionally applied to animatronic figures is compliant feedback. Compliant feedback reduces unintended shaking of the figure called "boing" (a problem for animatronics with fast movements and high masses). Boing can happen when the direction of an analog controlled move is instantly stopped or reversed. The result of this sudden change in velocity can cause part of the figure to oscillate a little bit. Compliant feedback is achieved by placing a load-sensing cell between each cylinder and rod end which produces an analog output that is proportional to the applied load. This allows the figure to "give" a little before stopping or reversing direction.

Things to Consider
Choosing Moves

Understanding and selecting the movements for an animated figure is probably the most mysterious aspect of animatronic figures for newcomers. This is largely because new buyers naturally reference their own movement abilities when trying to imagine what that will look like in an animatronic figure. Unfortunately, the available technology and budgets do not allow for this level of movement to be created.

The process by which movements are selected for animatronic figures typically involves defining the needs of the presentation, analyzing the budget, and then selecting those movements which are necessary to carry the presentation. Factors such as length of the show, number of media elements within the show, personality of the character, and required gestures of the figure are all factored into the decision making process.

The following list is an attempt to create a generalized hierarchy of animatronic movements. The first movements on the list are often the most important for an animatronic to have. As each animatronic exhibit or attraction is different, this hierarchy is simply a starting point for a discussion that should involve the buyer, show designer, and animatronic designer.

Mouth and eye blinks
The mouth and eye blinks are essential for creating a character that talks. A single digital mouth move can simulate most talking movements, and the blinking eyes are absolutely required to make the figure look natural.

Head turns and eye turns
Head and eye turns are typically the next movements added because they help the animatronic figure appear to have an awareness of its surroundings. The eyes make it appear to look around the room, and the head follows where the eyes lead, just like in humans.

Arm gesture
One or two moves are typically added to the arm or wrist before additional head moves are included. This allows the figure to make a few casual gestures or movements that make it appear that the body could move more if the figure so desired. The audience makes the same assumption about the figure that they make about a human or animal they walk up to: that it could move all of its body parts if it wanted; it just does not need to at that point. Typically the arm movements are concentrated in one arm, with the other arm being positioned so that the lack of movement does not appear unnatural – holding something, leaning on something, etc.

Body move
Once a body has been given the ability to gesture an arm, the next move added is typically a body lean or weight shift. This movement goes a long way toward creating personality in the figure, and also making the figure appear real. The personality comes from the ability of the figure to lean toward part of the audience when delivering a

Von Maur's WWII pilot utilizes a pose that gives the character a more relaxed, natural position, which also allows less movement throughout the body. Notice the binocular prop in his hand - a very effective way to hide the fact that his hands are not animated.

dramatic idea, or lean back when surprised or laughing. The increased realism comes from the appearance that the figure's body is mobile, and so it could walk away if it desired.

Head nods and tilts
Additional head moves are added to create personality for the figure. It can look up as if remembering something, it can tilt its head if curious about something and it can look down if it is sad.

Additional arm moves
These are moves that allow the figure to point at something, or make more sophisticated gestures than the couple of arm moves discussed above.

Additional body moves
These are moves in the torso area that help create a more dynamic presentation, and give the figure the ability to look more places around the room.

A word about a standing up effect
One of the movement combinations that customers often suggest is the ability to have a figure go from a sitting position to a standing position and back again. While this can be a nice effect, it is often not vital to the effectiveness of the presentation. And given the number of movements required to create the effect, the budget can often be better allocated to other movements.

Things to Consider
Maintenance

Characters
The maintenance required for an animated figure depends largely on the complexity of the figure and the type of actuators used. Most animatronic figures are created using industrial rated components, meaning they are rated for millions of cycles and greater loads than most characters produce. An exception to this is when servo motors are used, as their lifespan is still not as long as pneumatic or hydraulic cylinders.

The skeletal structure of the figures is steel, stainless steel, aluminum, or a combination of the three. When designed and programmed correctly, the skeletal structure should not fatigue or break.

Support Equipment
The support equipment, however, will require some maintenance from time to time:

Compressors
Pneumatic figures require a compressed air supply to actuate the cylinders. The oil levels should be checked weekly, and the water drained from the tank every few weeks. A compressor with low oil will overheat, blowing the seals, and sending damaging oil into the animatronic figure. Too much water in the tank will reduce the space available for compressed air, and increase the duty cycle, thereby wearing out the compressor sooner than its intended lifespan. Compressor maintenance can be performed by a layperson. It is similar to checking the oil in a car.

Hydraulic Pumps
Similar to air compressors, hydraulic pumps will need their fluids checked. Unlike compressors, however, they do not require water to be drained. Hydraulic pumps are a bit more involved than air compressors, and should have someone familiar with machinery maintain them.

Control Systems
Control systems are computer and circuit board based. As a result, they are susceptible to the same problems other electronic equipment is. Hard drives can fail, power surges can damage them, and overheating can cause them to perform erratically. The best maintenance that can be performed on them is to keep them clean and in a well ventilated area. When they do fail, it is usually possible to simply replace the faulty components and restore the show from a back-up file kept on a disc or spare drive.

Things to Consider
Definitions

Move/degree of freedom
This is the most basic animatronic action. An eye blink, for example, is one move. By combining several moves together realistic movement can be created. A wrist bend, elbow bend, and shoulder move all work together to create realistic arm movement.

Digital
This is the most basic and affordable move available. It has two positions. An eye blink, for example, is often a digital move - it is either open or closed (or on its way to one of those two positions). A digital move has a constant speed that does not change throughout the show.

Analog
This is a more advanced move than the digital move. Similar to a light dimmer, this move can stop anywhere along its path. A head turn is a typical use for an analog move. It can look to the left, look to the right, and can stop anywhere in between. This type of movement is also capable of moving fast one second, and slow the next.

Piston compressor
This is a standard compressor typically found in a hardware store. It is somewhat loud and should be kept away from visitor/guest areas. It does not require as much maintenance as other types of compressors, but should be checked at least once a month.

Silent compressor
This is a compressor that has a quiet motor similar to that of a refrigerator. It requires a regimented maintenance schedule, and is only used when a suitable space for a piston compressor cannot be found.

Air dryer
This is a machine that is plumbed between the air compressor and the character. It pulls most of the moisture out of the air before it is sent to the character. This extends the life of the character by reducing the potential for rust and corrosion.

Control system
Animatronic characters require some type of control system to synchronize their movements with the audio and any other show elements that may be used (video, lighting, special effects, curtains, etc.). In most cases, a PC based control system is used. This includes a customized computer with a monitor, keyboard, and some type of speaker system. This computer must be dedicated to operating the character, and cannot be used for other tasks.

The Brain fortune teller was wildly successful thanks to careful planning of personality, scripts, and voice long before production ever started.

The Process
Designing and Building an Animatronic Character

Animatronic characters are design driven. This means that the client and manufacturer typically establish what they want the character to look like and what they want it to do. This may be as simple as "we want a duck on a tricycle singing about ice cream" or as detailed as a set of engineered plans with a maquette. In either case, it's a starting point for the "dream versus budget tug-of-war" through which most projects progress.

Creating an animatronic character is a very intricate process that involves many fields of expertise. The art and technology involved in making animatronic characters is generally spread through a number of different departments including design and engineering, sculpting, mold-making, skin fabrication, painting and hairing, armature and movement development, hosing and final assembly, prop and scenic creation, costuming, sound production, special effect development, and programming. All of these departments are synchronized through a series of meetings and approval loops between the client and manufacturer.

The process all begins with an initial meeting to determine the project objective and audience profile. Establishing the specific purpose of the animatronic character is crucially important in assuring its ultimate success. During this design process, the client and manufacturer decide on the final appearance, the scale, the location of the moves, and the type of moves (analog or digital). Budget, timelines, checkpoints, and sign-offs are all established. Scriptwriting and voice talent selection are also areas that have been acknowledged and assigned for production. Once these variables are solidified, the actual character project moves into production. The following pages provide a quick tour through the various departments involved with the production of an animatronic figure.

The Process
Sculpting

The sculpting department is responsible for converting two-dimensional ideas into three-dimensional forms. The sculptor can work from photos, sketches, models, statues, video, and written descriptions. When sculpting a human head, the sculpting process starts with an armature appropriate for the size of the head. When sculpting a body or large shape (dinosaur), the sculptor usually starts with a carved foam understructure. This understructure may or may not be covered with clay, depending on the required detail. A body hidden beneath clothing does not need fine detail. A dinosaur, however, may require the fine detail clay permits.

A static butler sculpt in process has too extreme of an expression to easily animate.

There are three basic steps at which the sculpt is reviewed along the sculpting process: rough, detailed, textured.

A rough sculpt: the size and shape of the head have been established. Dominant features have been incorporated into the surface, but winkles and texture have not been. For head sculpts, the size of the nose, location of the eyes, weight in the cheeks, shape of the mouth, and expression are all evident (see sidebar: expressions for animated figures). For bodies and other sculpts, the general shape is approved.

The detailed sculpt: the sculpt is smoothed and the small details are added. For head sculpts, the transitions between features are blended and wrinkles are added. Approval at this point is for everything but the very subtle skin texture.

The textured sculpt: for human heads the sculpt has had the appropriate skin texture added. This is the last step before the sculpt enters the molding process, and is the last chance to change anything in the sculpt.

Expressions for animated figures

A couple of factors come into play when sculpting an expression for animated figures: 1) The face is usually sculpted in the *halfway* position. Meaning that the mouth is sculpted half open, the brow may be sculpted slightly raised if there is to be a brow move, etc. This can make it difficult for people to imagine what the finished figure will look like when the features are moved to their resting position on the final figure. 2) The character has to look natural throughout the entire presentation. A great big smile on a human figure may look really odd when the figure starts talking because the cheeks and lips are not often movements included in animated figures.

The Process
Molding and Casting

The plastics and resins department creates the molds and castings for each of the components in an animatronic figure.

Molding

The first step in translating a sculpt into the final animatronic figure is molding. Mold making is a process that is very time consuming and can be somewhat complicated. And because the sculpt is typically destroyed by the molding process, it is a job that has little room for error. Once created, most molds can be stored indefinitely in the proper atmospheric conditions.

The general methodology behind the molding process is to use a resin that will capture all of the detail of the sculpt when it hardens, and will have enough strength to survive multiple castings. Common casting materials include fiberglass, silicone, urethane, latex, and plaster. Depending on the sculpted piece, the molds can be hard, soft, single piece, multiple piece, reusable or one-time use molds. Once molded, the piece cannot be altered.

Casting

Once the mold is created, the appropriate material can be used to cast the piece. For animatronic figures, this is usually a silicone rubber for soft figures or gel coat and fiberglass for hard figures. Sometimes a core is used inside the mold to assure a specific thickness for the skin.

With some sculpts, the molding process is bypassed, and the necessary pieces are cast directly from the sculpt. Bodies are typically cast in this fashion because they do not require any detail if they are hidden beneath clothing. Fiberglass or similar material is laid over the foam sculpted body, then cut off and used as the final shell.

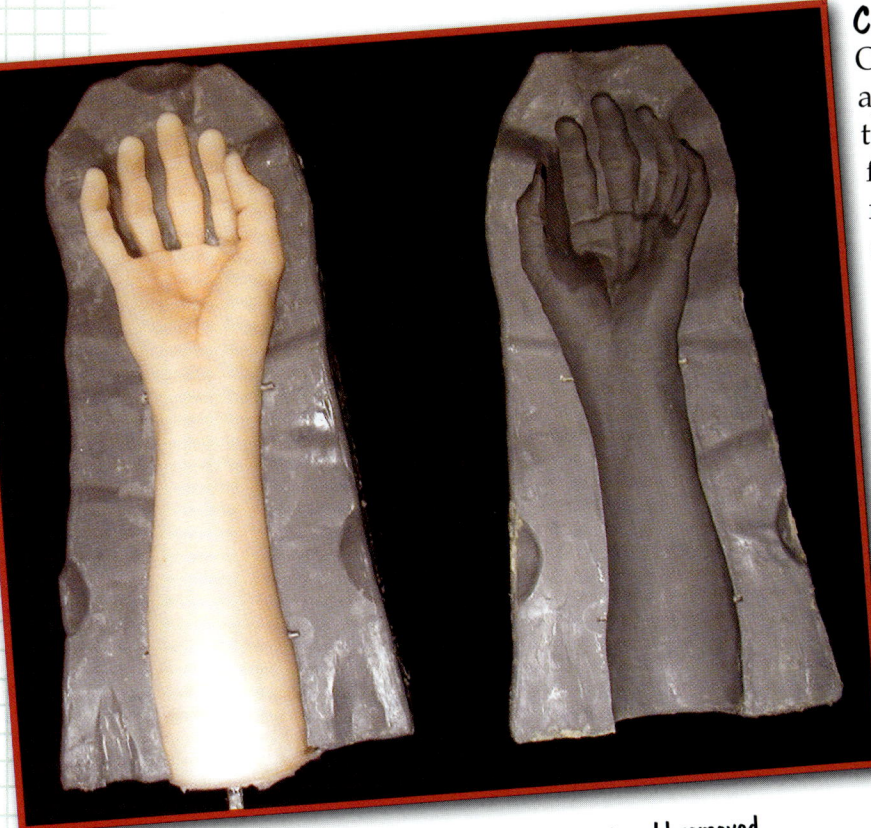

A silicone hand cast and one side of the two-part mold removed. Note the detail in the part of the mold to the right.

The Process
Fabrication & Machining

The fabrication department uses a combination of off-the-shelf and custom parts to create the moving components of the animatronic figure. Their challenge is to fit all of the necessary components within the confines of an acceptable appearance for the figure. In other words, an armature for a human animatronic with over 50 separate movements still has to fit within the confines of a typical human size and shape.

The design of an animatronic figure is based very much on the skeleton and muscle design that allows humans to walk around. A metal or composite skeleton is created with joints located at the proper locations. Cylinders or cables are then attached across those joints to allow the movement to be created. When pressure is applied to one side of the cylinder, it contracts. When it is applied to the other side of the cylinder, it expands.

The direction of the flow is typically controlled by one or two valves per cylinder. The control system triggers the valves to change the direction of air flow to apply pressure to the proper sides of the valves. Restrictors and flow controls in the air lines limit the amount of flow permitted through the hoses.

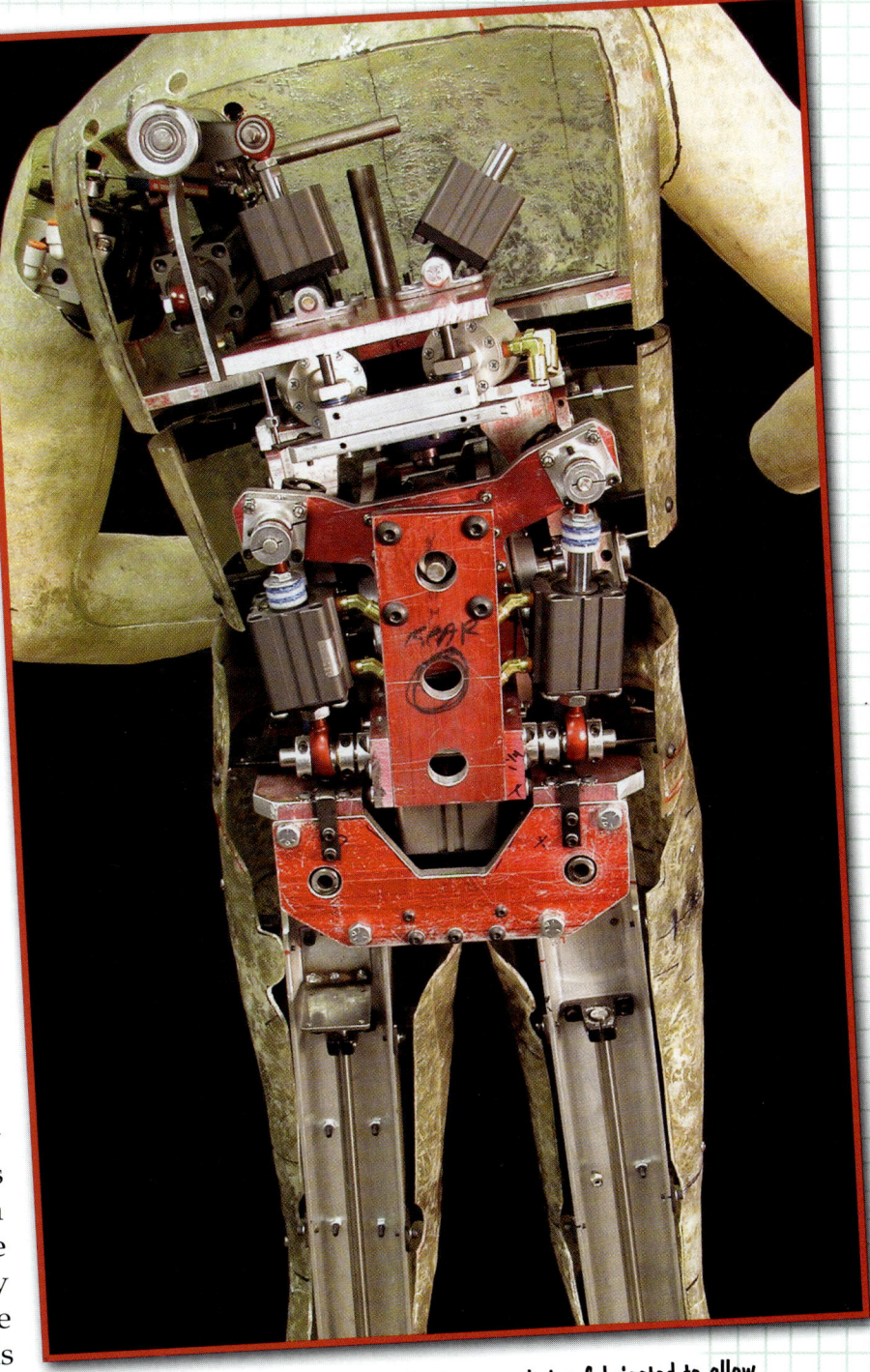

Human as the mechanisms are being fabricated to allow for 18 analog and 22 digital moves.

The Process
Scriptwriting and Audio

Scriptwriting for Animated Figures
Good scriptwriting is imperative to a successful presentation. One of the biggest mistakes buyers of animatronics make is to believe they should write the script for the figures simply because they know about the content. The results can be absolutely disastrous. A scriptwriter is able to combine the general ideas and content from the buyer with the proper blend of humor, personality, emotion and information. A scriptwriter who is comfortable writing for the specific animatronic application (entertainment, information, sales, etc.) can serve as an objective force, keeping the script from becoming too packed with mundane information or elements that do not move the story along. Once the script is written, everyone can take a look at it and make any modifications that are necessary.

Audio for Animated Figure Voices
There are three important rules when working with audio for animatronic figures:

1) Personality is vital.
Animatronic figures are basically stage performers. As such, they need to have an actors voice. Recording studios have stables of voice talent available with a variety of different styles. Depending on the character, some buyers try to use either the actual person, a family member, or someone working at the company. The problem is, those people are not actors, and as a result the presentation does not sound professional. The fact that it was a relative or important company executive is completely lost on the audience. Nobody will know who the voice was. They just hear someone who is obviously not an actor, and the entire suspension of disbelief is shattered.

2) Pacing is important.
Animatronic mouths are typically operated by digital cylinders, meaning they can not change speed if the voice changes speed. As a result, the voice talent must keep a very even speed as they read the scripts. The animatronic company can then set the mouth to the appropriate speed and the mouth can match the script. The voice talent should also not talk too fast, as the result is a mouth move that is so fast it does not look realistic.

3) Technical quality is a necessity.
The cost to record a voice is a relatively small cost in relation to the cost of an animated character. Never-the-less, this is a place where some buyers try to save money. The result is audio that has pops, is over driven, or even has noises in the background. All of these can ruin the impact of the animatronic presentation.

The Process
Figure Finishing and Costumes

Painting the Castings
The cast pieces must be prepped for painting. This includes cutting off the parting line, trimming the edges, and patching any holes or air bubble cavities. Each manufacturer has its own secret technique to achieve the right translucency and believable skin tones. Some painters sponge, some stipple, and some spray. In any event, the result is usually a very durable coloring that is resistant to rubbing off during routine cleaning and maintenance.

Hairing
There are several different methods to hair a figure, ranging from simply gluing a wig on, to inserting each hair into the head one by one. In most cases, the chosen method is directly related to the viewing distance and time of the audience. Usually the final method involves a combination of gluing on some of the hair in small patches, and poking in the hair along the hairline one hair at a time.

The Other Details
There are many other finishing details that help create a realistic figure. Eyes are typically colored with varying levels of red and yellow to make them match the age or look of the animatronic character. Teeth may be sculpted into the original sculpt, or may need to be added. Often just the front top teeth are added. Short fingernails are often part of the hand casting, so longer fingernails need to be added if the character requires them.

Costumes
Two aspects of an animatronic figure make immediate impact: the realism of the head, and the believability of the costume. The breadth of costume sources spreads from the local thrift store to custom sewn clothing made from antique fabrics and buttons. Additionally, the proper level of aging must be applied to match the scene. This includes misting the fabric with various colors and applying stains in the proper locations.

The ship-wrecked sailor with "weathered" clothing, bloodshot eyes and poked beard warns visitors entering a dark ride at Europa Park. Depsite his caricature appearance, he was still very realistic.

The Process
Control Systems

Control systems cause everything to happen for an animatronic figure and its support media. There are literally hundreds of ways to control animatronic shows ranging from simple relay panels for live operation to very sophisticated PLC systems. Most animatronic companies, however, tend to either use their own proprietary control system or gravitate toward a couple of suppliers building control systems specifically for animatronic figures.

The control system is basically a means by which to store the media and movement cues so they are synchronized when they are played back. This may be as simple as saving a single audio file and movement cue file that play back together when a button is pushed, or it can be as complicated as synchronizing audio, video, movement, lighting, and special effects cues for an entire theater show or ride.

The programming of the figures can be performed by building the movement cue program while listening to the audio in real time, or it can be done *off-line* by assigning certain moves to certain points along a visual timeline. While each programmer has his or her own philosophy on how best to create a realistic looking program, most will start with the mouth move, if the figure is talking, before moving onto the other head moves, then the arm and body moves.

The playback for control systems can be triggered by a timer, motion sensor, input from another control system, push button, SMPTE, MIDI, DMX, or just about any other signal imaginable. A control system can also be operated live, with actors and operators talking directly through the figures while controlling them with a push button panel or joystick.

"Thid and Thtan's Ithe Cream Cart" utilizes a touchscreen to communicate with the control system which activates the characters, cart lights and other effects when users touch designated areas on the screen.

The Process
Installation

Animatronic figures are typically one of the last elements of an exhibit or attraction to be installed. The installation process can be as simple as anchoring the figure into place and plugging it in, or it can require more elaborate integration with other systems. Aside from the figure, there are site preparations that need to be completed long before the animatronic figures arrive.

Air Supply
A supply line from the compressor/dryer to the character locations must be run prior to the installation of the figures. Ideally, this is a copper pipe installed by a plumber, with a ball valve at the character location. The animatronic install team will then tap into the end of the ball valve with the appropriate fittings to tie in the character.

Occasionally, polyethylene hose will be used for the entire run, particularly if the characters are being installed in an existing building that requires snaking the supply line through walls and ceilings. The down side of polyethylene hose is that it can kink, and can be punctured far easier than copper piping.

Electrical Supply
Most animatronic figures require a power supply at the control system location, but not the character location. A cable is then run from the control system to the characters with the required power to fire the valves.

Control Cables
A control cable will need to be run from the characters to the control system. This is typically a low voltage cable that should be run along the shortest possible route.

Other Cables
There are other cables that should be run when the wiring is installed. These include cables for speakers, lighting, motion detectors, push buttons, and similar devices.

Mounting
Animatronic figures are typically mounted to wood stages or cement floors. This is a relatively easy process typically involving bolts or tap-cons. When the figures are mounted to a wall or ceiling, a structural engineer hired by the owner or general contractor must sign-off on the weight and mounting method of the figures.

Final Programming Tweaks
While programming of a character's movement often takes place before it ships, there are times when final programming must be performed on site. This is a relatively easy process, but can involve coordination with the suppliers of the lighting, scenery, other show action equipment, special effects, and any media.

The Process
Supporting Media

Willy Getdere and his Amazing Time Machine utilized a proprietary control system providing movement which was synchronized to a DVD player, allowing 5.1 Dolby Digital Audio and high resolution video to be incorporated.

While animatronic figures are perfectly capable of being standalone presentations, they are often combined with other supporting elements to create a more powerful experience. Sometimes the animatronic companies supply these support elements themselves, sometimes they sub-contract these elements, and sometimes they simply work with other companies hired by the buyer. The following are several of the elements commonly found with animatronics:

Themeing and Sets
Creating an environment around the character helps frame the presentation for the audience, preparing them for what they are about to see. It can also help the audience suspend their disbelief, and become more a part of the show.

Video
Often used in exhibits that are trying to communicate specific information or a concept, video can be synchronized to the animatronic figure to illustrate what is being discussed. It is also used in several CircleTheater attractions that have an animatronic host for the video image projected in a 360 degree screen around the audience.

Lighting
Lighting is often used to help make the attraction or exhibit look better. It is also a great tool to direct the attention of the audience to a certain place at a certain time. This allows the show creators to reveal different aspects of the show at different times, thereby keeping the interest of the audience.

Special Effects
Smoke machines, bubbles, lasers, animated props, and a variety of other special effects are very commonly used with animatronic figures. They help keep the audience's interest.

Interactive Panels
Pushbuttons, touchscreens, and other types of interactive mechanisms allow the audience to participate in the experience, often increasing the impact of the presentation.

Thomas Edison quizzes passersby about animatronic concepts via a touchscreen interactive which was integrated with the animation control system.

Credits

The following companies and people have not only contributed to the success of the projects featured in this book, but also our understanding of animatronics.

1220 Exhibits
American Girl
American National Fish and Wildlife Museum
The Avampato Science Center
Neil Baker
Allen Boerger
Jim Bonaminio
Bowling Green State University
The Canadian Niagara Group
The Chisholm Trail Museum
COSI Columbus
COSI Studio
Design Craftsmen
Michael Dicienzo
Tom Dowd
EarlyWorks Museum Complex
Mike Edgren
ESPN
Europa Park
Exhibit Concepts
Ken Feingold
D.R. Finley
Forrec Limited
Genflex Roofing Systems
Grand Dental
Johnny Gruber
Steve Hanson
Dan Hoffman
Garner Holt
Honeywell
Jekyll and Hyde Restaurants
Johnson Hospital
Jungle Jim's International Market
Mark and MaryAnn Kashube
King's City
Bob Lammers
M3 Marketing
John March
Marvin's Marvelous Mechanical Museum
Shane McCall
MGM Grand Casino
Midmark
Frank Murphy
National Wild Turkey Federation
Zvi Oren
Ian Paul
Doug Powhida
Ride and Show Engineering
Ava Ritter
Teit Ritzau
Bob Rogers
Jack Rouse Associates
Rubbermaid
The Sands Hotel
Taipei Astronimical Museum
The Toledo Zoo
United Exhibits
Vacuflo of Ohio
Von Maur
Joe Wisne
John Wood
Cartho Bennett
Pete Carsillo

The Authors

Rodney Heiligmann, Ph.D.
Rodney is a professor of visual communication at Bowling Green State University in Bowling Green, Ohio. He has taught exhibit design and media production for the past 9 years. He has a Masters degree in Education and a Ph.D. in Communication. Rodney is also a partner of LifeFormations, where he serves as president. Prior industry experience stretches from a stint at Walt Disney World as a Jungle Cruise skipper, through project development and management roles, to leadership positions in professional organizations.

Gene W. Poor, Ph.D.
Gene has a Ph.D. in Education. He is a professor of visual communication at Bowling Green State University, where he developed the Visual Communication Technology program 25 years ago. He started Lifeformations in 1991 after consulting in the animatronics industry for over ten years. Poor has authored a number of books and articles on animatronics, communication technology, and training and development.

Travis Gillum, M.Ed.
Travis has a Bachelor of Science degree in Visual Communication Technology and a Masters degree in Education from Bowling Green State University. He has been teaching visual communication courses ranging from video production and senior synthesis to digital imaging for the past 4 years. Travis is a partner of Lifeformations with current responsibilities of project management and media development as well as assisting with the direction of production.

Grant Marsh - legendary river boat captain.